D1252988

In-Laws

Getting Along with Your Other Family

Ron & Jorie Kincaid

InterVarsity Press
Downers Grove, Illinois

InterVarsity Press® is the book-publishing division of InterVarsity Christian Fellowship®, a student movement active on campus at hundreds of universities, colleges and schools of nursing in the United States of America, and a member movement of the International Fellowship of Evangelical Students. For information about local and regional activities, write Public Relations Dept., InterVarsity Christian Fellowship, 6400 Schroeder Rd., P.O. Box 7895, Madison, WI 53707-7895.

Cover photograph: Kevin Moan/SuperStock
ISBN 0-8308-1954-1

Printed in the United States of America

Library of Congress Cataloging-in-Publication Data

Kincaid, Ron.
   In-laws: getting along with your other family/Ron and Jorie
Kincaid.
      p.   cm.
   Includes bibliographical references.
   ISBN 0-8308-1954-1 (pbk.: alk. paper)
      1. Parents-in-law—United States.   2. Interpersonal relations—
United States.   I. Kincaid, Jorie.   II. Title.
HQ759.8.K56   1996
646.7'8—dc20   96-16812
                                                CIP

| 18 | 17 | 16 | 15 | 14 | 13 | 12 | 11 | 10 | 9 | 8 | 7 | 6 | 5 | 4 | 3 | 2 | 1 |
| 11 | 10 | 09 | 08 | 07 | 06 | 05 | 04 | 03 | 02 | 01 | 00 | 99 | 98 | 97 | 96 |

*We dedicate this book to
our parents and parents-in-law,
Arnold and Anna Hultgren
and
Warren and Dorothy Kincaid*

*We wish to thank Sheri Nee and Cynthia Bunch-Hotaling
for their help in shaping this manuscript into a book.*

*While all the stories in this book are true,
to protect those who have shared their experiences with us,
we have changed the names and some of the details in these accounts.*

*While the two of us worked closely together on the ideas
in this book, for the sake of continuity
most of the stories are told in Ron's voice.*

1
How
Problems
Begin

A young woman wrote to Ann Landers: My sweetheart and I have decided to marry. Dan wants to elope. I can understand why. He knows that his mother and sister both despise me and that I don't want to invite them to our wedding. Dan's mother ruined his sister's wedding because she hated the groom. The problem is that I am my father's only child, and I feel it is important for him to walk me down the aisle. I don't want a lonely elopement, but neither do I want to suffer through a terribly tense wedding.

Weary in the West

(P.S. I can't stand his family.)

Here is the reply she got:

Dear Weary:

Have the wedding. You'll be glad you did. And please try to improve your relationship with Dan's family. Battling with in-laws puts a dead hand on a marriage from the start.[1]

Ann Landers was right on target. Few things put more strain on a marriage than tensions with in-laws.

Research confirms that the most complicated relationship people have is the in-law relationship. Experts agree that three-quarters of all married couples have problems with their in-laws.[2] A young mother told us, "My relationship with my mother-in-law is the most difficult relationship I have encountered in my thirty years." Many men and women were totally unprepared for the anxiety and problems they have encountered with their in-laws. We began to study this issue and realized how many people struggle in relationships with their in-laws, be it with a mother-, father-, son-, daughter-, brother-, sister-, grandfather- or grandmother-in-law.

Difficulties with in-laws are not new.

A poor farm boy, Harry S. Truman, married the rich girl from town. As a result, he had to endure her disapproving mother. The woman didn't think any man was good enough for her daughter—especially a plain-spoken youth from the sticks—and made no attempt to hide her feelings. The young couple couldn't afford a home of their own, so they moved in with the bride's mother—and they stayed married for thirty-three years! Even when the couple moved from Independence, Missouri, to Kansas City, and later to the White House, Harry Truman's mother-in-law, Madge Gates Wallace, was still there, ruling the dinner table. "It was very hard on my father," Truman's daughter, Margaret, said years later. "But he made it his business to get along because he loved my mother." Out of love for his wife, Truman was determined to get along with his mother-in-law.

Winston Churchill's "darling Clementine" also learned early that she had married not just her husband but also his strong-willed mother. When she and Winston returned from their honeymoon, the young bride discovered that Lady Randolph Churchill had completely redecorated the couple's new home in a style far fancier than Clementine had planned.

Neither the Trumans nor the Churchills, however, suffered the in-law wars that beset President Ulysses S. Grant and his wife, Julia Dent Grant. Julia's father, a wealthy planter who often stayed with the Grants in the White House, had made no secret of what he thought of Grant when the young lieutenant married Julia. And the president's father, Jesse, who also often stayed at the White House, didn't like Julia's father. When the two fathers-in-law conversed, it was usually to exchange insults.[3]

Difficulties with in-laws even go back to early Bible times. Laban didn't want to marry off his beautiful daughter Rachel before marrying off his oldest, "weak-eyed" daughter, Leah. So he tricked Jacob by giving him Leah instead of Rachel, even though Jacob had already labored seven years for Rachel. Any father would want both of his daughters to be happily married, especially in that culture. Knowing that one daughter was especially beautiful and the other had a physical weakness, it would be natural for a father to do what he could to help his physically challenged daughter. But out of his fear to protect his oldest daughter, Laban made poor choices regarding an equally important relationship— that with his son-in-law. When Jacob later asked to leave, Laban schemed up ways to detain him, probably because he feared losing his daughters and grandchildren. Rather than granting Jacob freedom to leave, Laban tried to control his son-in-law by delaying his departure. But the longer Jacob and his family remained, the more strained their relationship became.

Numerous couples have confessed to us in counseling that their greatest source of tension is their relationships with their in-laws. Seldom do couples identify this concern when they are first engaged, but about the time when invitations are sent, wedding showers are held and details of the ceremony are planned, the couple begins to realize that opinions are surfacing and feelings are being stepped on. By the week of the wedding, simple parent-child relationships have turned into complex anxiety struggles. The bride may be crying, "Oh, why can't Mom understand?" and the groom may be asking, "What did I do that upset them so much?" Caught off guard, the couple may unintentionally become a party to a conflict that cuts deeply into the emotions of both the couple and their parents.

Jim and Linda, an engaged couple, told us they anticipated no problems in their marriage, but they expressed some concern about potential in-law troubles. Jim called his mom two to three times each week. Because his dad had died suddenly not long before, Jim felt responsible to take care of his mother. Watching out for his mother was compassionate and commendable, but the problem was that his mother made lots of critical statements about Linda and was constantly passing judgment on her. Whenever she felt Jim was catering more to Linda's wishes than to her own, she pouted until she got her way.

While planning the wedding, Linda decided that alcohol would be served at the rehearsal dinner. Jim's staunch Southern Baptist mother, realizing that the rehearsal dinner was the groom's family's responsibility, stated vehemently that there would be no alcohol at the dinner. Linda asked Jim to speak to his mother about the issue. Jim preferred to give in to his mother's wishes rather than make a big deal out of it. Linda felt that he was more concerned about his mother's feelings than her own.

The Pain Goes Both Ways
Difficulty between in-laws is not limited to the feelings of frustration that

children-in-law feel toward parents-in-law. We have counseled numerous parents grieving over a broken relationship with a son- or daughter-in-law. They want so badly to be on track with their children and want to be closely tied to their son- or daughter-in-law, but they feel that somewhere the family connection is derailing.

How many parents-in-law are abused by insensitive children who expect Grandma and Grandpa to care for the grandchildren? We know there are too many to count. Why should a mother or mother-in-law be made to feel pressured into "volunteering" to baby-sit so her daughter or daughter-in-law can go back to work, go shopping or work out regularly? Many of the younger generation are guilty of imposing on their in-laws this way.

Some grandmas *want* to baby-sit. Some do not. Some want to do it once in a while, or for a short period of time, or for one child at a time. Not many want to be on call all the time! Sadly, too many young couples consider grandparent child care their right instead of a gift. Relationships are strained when this issue is abused.

Madeline was abused in this way. Her husband died early in their retirement years. Madeline's daughter-in-law, Kathy, was exhausted from the pressures of raising several preschoolers; she began asking Madeline to relieve her. At first it was just so she could shop without the hindrance of several little ones sitting in the grocery cart. But gradually Kathy began showing up unannounced to leave the children at Grandma's—and returning late, sometimes hours after the time they had agreed on. She reasoned to herself that Madeline was lonely and needed something to fill up her time.

Madeline, a gracious, quiet-spoken woman, felt helpless. She was hesitant to confront Kathy and risk damaging their relationship. Yet she resented being taken advantage of.

Madeline needed time to grieve. She needed to spend time with peers; she needed to become involved in activities and ministry outside her home. She had faithfully raised her children and had looked forward to retirement as a time to travel and experience new adventures not possible while she had been restrained by small children and her husband's work. Although her husband was now gone, her needs and dreams had not left with him. Sensitive children should have looked beyond their own needs to consider hers and not abuse her kindness.

Most children grow up accustomed to having their parents meet their needs. As adult children grow in maturity and godliness, they recognize that the "taking" role needs to change—it is time to look for the right ways to *give* to parents and parents-in-law, rather than just expecting to receive from them.

So many people face tensions with in-laws that we tend to joke about it. We use humor as a means of relieving tension. Some people figure they must either laugh about their in-laws or cry. Such humor can come in the form of a snide remark by a husband about his wife's parents, a sarcastic retort by a wife about her husband's family or a joke passed around at a neighborhood party.

Billy's maternal grandmother had just come for a visit, and he was ecstatic. "How long can you stay, Gramma?" he asked.

"For two weeks," was her reply.

"Oh, goody, now Daddy can do his trick! It's a trick I've never seen anyone do before."

"What trick is that?" Gramma asked.

"Well," answered Billy, "Daddy said that if you stayed for a whole week, he'd climb the walls."[4]

Getting along with in-laws isn't a laughing matter. In his book *What Wives Wish Their Husbands Knew About Women,* James Dobson cites conflict with in-laws as one of the top ten sources of depression in women.

And tension with in-laws is not limited to the traditional husband and wife and two sets of parents. An increasing number of people today, due to divorces, remarriages and blended families, find they have to relate to new sets of in-laws *and* still struggle with former ones.

A young widower, whose wife had died of cancer in her mid-thirties, subsequently remarried. He confided to us that the toughest thing for him and his new wife to deal with in their marriage was their relationship with his former in-laws. His previous wife's parents, quite naturally, wanted to continue to see their grandchildren. But their visits made his wife and him uncomfortable. The former in-laws also wanted their grandchildren to come and stay with them for several weeks each summer. He and his wife did not like being separated from their kids for such long periods of time. Yet when they turned down the invitations or tried to shorten the length of the children's visits, the grandparents got very upset. The young couple found that the ongoing relationship with his former in-laws put great stress on their marriage.

Problematic relations with in-laws leave thousands of people with feelings of hopelessness and despair. You don't have to experience defeat with your in-laws, however. This book is our attempt to offer you new hope for restarting or restoring your relationships with your in-laws. We have both struggled at times in our relationships with our parents-in-law; we understand the feelings of exasperation regarding in-law relationships. We do not offer theoretical solutions to theoretical problems; rather, we offer real-life solutions to real-life situations. We also include life-changing principles from God's Word that have been proven through the test of time to revolutionize relationships.

Perhaps we should begin by identifying some of the most common problems found in in-law relationships.

The Freeze

One woman shared with us that her parents disliked her husband so much that they told her he was no longer invited to any family get-togethers. Their reasoning went something like this: "Got a son-in-law you don't like? Freeze him out. Pretend he doesn't exist." In response the daughter informed her parents that if he was not invited, she would not be coming either. So the two families cut off nearly all contact.

When Bob and Jill got married, they anticipated no in-law problems. But over time it became apparent that Bob's parents really didn't accept Jill. Whenever they sent a letter or gift, it was addressed only to Bob. When they called, they wanted to talk only to Bob. If Bob wasn't home, they expressed their disappointment and hung up quickly. They never asked how Jill was doing. Why not? In their minds their relationship with their daughter-in-law was not nearly as important as their relationship with their son. They always took great care to make a big deal over Bob's birthday and the grandkids' birthdays, taking time to visit, but Jill's birthday was conspicuously overlooked. Occasionally she received a birthday card, but never a phone call or visit. Whenever they visited, it was obvious that they were interested in seeing only Bob and the grandchildren. Jill felt like a nonperson in their presence. She clearly received the numerous nonverbal messages that they did not want a daughter—at least not her!

The Gift

Bill and Becky were nearly penniless when they married. Bill did not follow his father's footsteps into medicine, but settled for a relatively low-paying job. When their first child was born, Becky stayed home to be with the baby. It became obvious to Bill's parents that if Bill and Becky were ever to own a home they would need financial assistance. The parents loaned them money to make a down payment.

Bill and Becky were overjoyed with their new house. But it soon became apparent that the gift had come with strings attached. Since Bill's parents had helped them get into a house, they assumed that their assistance gave them the right to counsel them on all their purchases. And if they didn't like a decision the kids made as to interior decorating or landscaping, they did not hesitate to let it be known. Finally, after a couple of years of home ownership at the price of constant advice from Bill's parents, Bill and Becky sold their home and gave Bill's parents the down-payment money back. They felt the loss of their home was worth the sacrifice in order to buy back their freedom.

Dick and Dana had been married several years when they decided that Dick should go back to school for a graduate degree. Since they had little money, Dana's parents offered to pick up Dick's tuition. Yet after several months Dick and Dana became aware that Dana's parents resented the fact that Dick was not working and providing for Dana. Dick and Dana soon realized that the gift was hurting their relationship with her parents.

The Critic
John's parents didn't like any of the girls he dated during high school and college. When he began dating Mary, whom he later married, they made no secret of their disappointment. "Why don't you date others?" they asked bluntly. "Why don't you date a Jewish girl? Why are you dating someone from a lower social class?" Mary's father was a blue-collar worker, so Mary had grown up light years away from John's lifestyle as a physician's son. Because Mary was from a different social circle, John's parents assumed she was less intelligent. They once suggested that John go to a movie with his brother instead of with Mary, because "it's a movie she wouldn't understand." And when discussing wedding plans with Mary, John's mother recommended to her that she look for

17

her wedding dress at a garage sale! Mary was devastated, but because of her love for John she tried to suppress her hurt over the condescending statements.

John's parents demonstrated their displeasure by refusing to come to the wedding ceremony because it was not being held in a Jewish synagogue. They did manage to come up with a wedding gift, however . . . for John. They bought him a new car, but were careful to leave Mary's name off the card. Mary was beside herself, but desiring to be a good daughter-in-law, she sent a handwritten thank-you note for the car. However, instead of helping to repair the relationship, she lost further ground. John's dad notified them that she had misspelled a word!

John decided that enough was enough, and he confronted his parents. It didn't go well. His mom and dad became defensive and yelled that his statements were crazy. John yelled back. They didn't speak again for three months.

When John and Mary's first child was born, tensions between the couples resurfaced in a big way. The young couple's decision to dedicate their baby and raise the child in a Christian church rather than in the Jewish faith met with sharp criticism.

Mary confessed to us that after all the hurtful things her parents-in-law had said and done to her, she would rather die than leave her child in their care. She feels guilty about her feelings, but she does not want to communicate to her in-laws that their actions are acceptable by allowing them to spend time with their grandchild. John and Mary have resigned themselves to a poor relationship with their in-laws, with no resolution in sight. They feel dejected and defeated because no matter what they do, they never measure up to the in-laws' standards.

The Intrusion
Just a few months after Ron and Sarah were married, Ron was diagnosed

with terminal cancer. When Ron became so sick that he could not be left home alone, his parents offered to come live with them to help with Ron while Sarah was at work. At first their help was greatly appreciated, but after a while their constant presence became oppressive to Sarah. Her in-laws were with them at each meal. Every night they sat together in their tiny apartment's living room. Sarah hated having so little time alone with Ron.

Rick and Molly had been married nine years when Rick was involved in a serious car accident. Molly turned to her parents for help in paying the bills and caring for her two young children. Her parents pitched in for almost a year, and their daily involvement continued long after Rick had recovered and returned to work.

When Rick protested to Molly about her parents' intrusiveness in their marriage, she defended them. "We can't just push them away," she said. "They were there for us, and I can't hurt their feelings now." Only after her parents barged in uninvited a few times did Molly agree to speak to them and tell them that she and Rick needed their freedom back.

Lack of Love

Why do so many people struggle with their in-laws? What causes the dissension? We're convinced that the number-one reason people have problems with in-laws is *lack of love*. When all the sources of disagreement have been aired, all the verbal grenades have been thrown and the smoke clears, the single greatest reason people flounder in their relationships with their in-laws is the failure to love.

The bride who wrote to Ann Landers was so afraid that her in-laws were going to ruin her wedding that she did not love them enough to invite them to the ceremony. The parents who would not give their son their blessing feared that he was making a poor choice in a wife and refused to love his bride. The lonely widow thought she could keep her son by withholding love from his fiancée, criticizing her and pouting whenever he showed preference for his bride-to-be.

As we shall see, there are a number of reasons why people fail to love their in-laws. One reason is *fear* of rejection or of being hurt. We will examine these fears in chapter two. Another reason we lack love for our in-laws may be that we suffer from a *low self-concept.* We shrink back from reaching out in love for others because we do not feel good about ourselves and do not want to risk failure. We will consider this in chapter three. Chapter four probes the failure to apply the biblical principle of *leaving* our parents when we marry and *cleaving* to our spouse. Still another enemy of love toward in-laws is the *urge to control.* We have a difficult time loving others if we always have to be in control of our relationships. We will consider this problem in chapter five.

Poor communication is a constant frustration to love. Chapter six discusses how to improve communication with our in-laws. *Unresolved or mismanaged anger* is an unhealthy pattern that will eat away at our ability to love our in-laws. We will look at ways to manage anger in chapter seven. Chapter eight deals with still another problem that can tear away at our resolve to love our in-laws: *disagreements over parenting and the role of grandparents.* In chapter nine we will contemplate the issue of *care for elderly in-laws.* Disagreement about how to care for elderly parents can be a source of disharmony in marriage and in-law relationships.

Marriage brings together two families—families that often have very different ways of dealing with problems. Although we believe that careful attention to the principles we lay out in this book will help you substantially improve your relationship with your in-laws, we also admit that there may be some situations where there is such overwhelming dysfunction that the people involved can never hope to realize health and wholeness in their relationships.

We do, however, hope that strong, healthy relationships with in-laws can be attainable. One father writes,

> Our parents did not have a good relationship with their parents, and we have not had a good relationship with my parents. In our marriage, it has been Carol's biggest challenge to get along with her in-laws. We have decided not to let this happen with our children. We have made a choice to have a good relationship with our son-in-law and daughter-in-law. We don't want our sins to pass down to our children. With the Lord's help, we will break this chain.

If there has been a history of unrest with in-laws in your family, it doesn't have to continue. The generational chain of disharmony can be broken. If we practice loving our in-laws just as Christ loves us, we can reduce the friction that may exist. The solution lies not in ourselves but in the God who made us. Only as we turn to him and rely on the power of the Holy Spirit can we learn to love as God loves and become the kind of people who can experience harmony in our relationships with our in-laws.

An Example to Follow

If you live in fear of being criticized or taken advantage of by your in-laws and worry that your situation is hopeless, you can learn how to love them by looking to the examples of the biblical writers, who were no strangers to fear and hopelessness. They wrote of it often.

King David writes in Psalm 55,

> My heart is in anguish within me;
>> the terrors of death assail me.
> Fear and trembling have beset me;
>> horror has overwhelmed me. (vv. 4-5)

David knew fear. Fear of enemies. Fear of death. His mind was filled with worries. How did he deal with his fears?

I said, "Oh, that I had the wings of a dove!
  I would fly away and be at rest—
I would flee far away
  and stay in the desert;
I would hurry to my place of shelter,
  far from the tempest and storm." (vv. 6-8)

In the face of fear, David wants to fly away and be at rest. He wants to flee to a deserted place away from the tempest. Isn't that what we all would like to do when we are troubled? We want to get away—to remove ourselves from the source of pain.

He continues,

If an enemy were insulting me,
  I could endure it;
if a foe were raising himself against me,
  I could hide from him.
But it is you, a man like myself,
  my companion, my close friend,
with whom I once enjoyed sweet fellowship
  as we walked with the throng at the house of God. (vv. 12-14)

If David's problems were with enemies, he could have endured it. But he was living in fear of friends who had turned into traitors. We can feel his distress. David's heart bled for the man he had so completely trusted. More than likely he speaks of Ahithophel, his trusted counselor from Giloh. Sweet had been the fellowship that they had enjoyed on occasion; arm in arm they went to the sanctuary in festal processions. This was not an enemy, but a close associate and intimate acquaintance. To know that such a one had turned against him hurt deeply.

One reason criticism from in-laws can be so hurtful is that we don't expect them to be our enemies. They are family. We count on them to be on our side. We hope they will build us up, not tear us down.

Notice how David handles his fears.

Confuse the wicked, O Lord, confound their speech. . . .

Let death take my enemies by surprise;

    let them go down alive to the grave,

      for evil finds lodging among them. (vv. 9, 15)

David asks God to see to it that his enemies, who have no regard for God, receive their just due. Reading between the lines and comparing with other events in David's life, we find a commitment by David not to take vengeance into his own hands. God says, "It is mine to avenge; I will repay" (Deut 32:35). David is going to trust God to set everything straight.

It is probably unfair to compare our in-laws to the "wicked" whom David describes here. Our in-laws may even be Christians. But we all know that Christian parents- and children-in-law can behave in very un-Christian ways. When in-laws have hurt you, everything inside you may feel like getting back at them. It is far better, however, for you to tell God that you will not take vengeance into your own hands. Ask him to help you treat them as Christ would have you treat them.

David takes his most important step in overcoming fear in his next statement:

But I call to God,

    and the LORD saves me.

Evening, morning and noon

    I cry out in distress,

    and he hears my voice. . . .

Cast your cares on the LORD

    and he will sustain you;

      he will never let the righteous fall. (vv. 16-17, 22)

In the face of fear, David turns to God. He cries out to the Lord for help. He casts his fears upon God. He trusts God to take care of him. He is confident that God will sustain him and never let the righteous fall.

Are you afraid of losing your son or daughter to a spouse who is immature and seems to be pulling your child away from you? Or do you fear that your mate may feel closer to his or her parents than to you? Are you afraid of the disapproval you feel in every conversation with your difficult in-law? Tell God your worries. Be brutally honest with God about your fears. Tell him you are willing to treat your in-laws as Christ would have you treat them. They may not respond in kind, but tell God that you will put your trust in him and leave the results to him.

Questions for Reflection or Discussion

1. Why do you think so many people have problems getting along with their in-laws?

2. The authors say, "The number-one reason people have problems with in-laws is lack of love." Do you agree or disagree with this assessment? Why or why not?

3. Of the four categories of in-law problems—the freeze, the gift, the critic and the intrusion—with which do you most identify? Why?

4. "Lack of love for in-laws is frequently caused by fear." Do you agree or disagree with this statement? Why or why not?

5. Read Psalm 55:1-15. How did David deal with his fears?

6. What insight from this chapter was most helpful to you?

2

Love:
The Key
That Unlocks
the Door

O*ne of the finest examples in* Scripture of how to treat in-laws is found in the book of Ruth. As the story begins, we find that a man from Bethlehem named Elimelech, his wife, Naomi, and their two sons went to live in Moab because of a severe famine in their own land. But Elimelech died, and Naomi was left with her two sons. Each of them took Moabite women as wives. After ten years, her sons also died. Naomi found herself not only widowed but bereft of her two sons.

Naomi decided to return to Bethlehem. She told her daughters-in-law, Orpah and Ruth, to go back to their home and find new husbands. Orpah agreed, but Ruth clung to her mother-in-law and said,

Don't urge me to leave you or to turn back from you. Where you go

I will go, and where you stay I will stay. Your people will be my people and your God my God. Where you die I will die, and there I will be buried. May the LORD deal with me, be it ever so severely, if anything but death separates you and me. (Ruth 1:16-17)

Ruth was willing to leave her homeland and her people and even to worship Naomi's God, the God of Israel—because of her love for her mother-in-law.

So Naomi took Ruth back to Judah. When they arrived in Israel, Naomi helped Ruth find a husband, Boaz. Boaz told Ruth that one reason he was attracted to her was her attitude toward her mother-in-law.

I've been told all about what you have done for your mother-in-law since the death of your husband—how you left your father and mother and your homeland and came to live with a people you did not know before. May the LORD repay you for what you have done. May you be richly rewarded by the LORD, the God of Israel, under whose wings you have come to take refuge. (2:11-12)

Why was Ruth so irresistibly drawn to her mother-in-law? Our hunch is that it was because Naomi loved her. If Naomi had feelings of jealousy when her son married, she rooted them out and loved Ruth as if she were her own daughter. Gone was the judgmental and critical spirit that typifies many in-law relationships. Ruth could trust Naomi.

The Power of Love

Love is the key to your relationship with your in-laws. It was true in Ruth's day and is still true today. One woman writes:

I have the most wonderful mother-in-law in the world. I have thought about why I adore her as I do, and it really is because she loves me very much. She has never spoken a critical word to me or about me. As you know, in large families everyone repeats everything being said, and the only thing I have ever heard someone say about me coming from the mouth of my mother-in-law is that I am her angel. Notice that the mother-in-law loves her daughter-in-law, and then the daughter-in-law responds in kind. The first step is crucial: *Someone has to choose to love.* That love is God's appointed means for breaking down all barriers. How different our society would be if all mothers-in-law called their daughters-in-law their angels and vice versa. Wow!

In preparation for a memorial service for one of our church members, we asked the family to share with us their special memories of their husband and father. The two daughters-in-law and son-in-law told us that he treated all of them as his own family. One shared that he had once said to her, "I sure hope your dad doesn't mind how much I love you." Isn't that great? He loved her as his own daughter and was openly expressive of it.

The other daughter-in-law told us that any time her father-in-law talked to her husband on the phone, he always instructed him to give her a big kiss. He was so consistent about giving this instruction that as soon as her husband got off the phone, she would come running for her kiss. The love he had for his son-in-law and two daughters-in-law caused all three of them to adore him.

I don't know where he learned the wisdom of loving his in-laws, but I wouldn't be surprised to find that he learned it from his parents. Be aware that the way you treat your parents-in-law makes an impression on your children—and it can set the stage for how they and their spouses will someday treat you!

A member of our church told us that his parents were frustrated by the disrespect they received from their other son and his rudeness toward his in-laws. "I don't know why they should be surprised," he added. "I've noticed for years how poorly my dad treats my mom's parents. He makes snide remarks about them all the time. My brother has just picked up on it. He learned it from my dad." Learning to love in-laws can be modeled by parents.

It is also taught in Scripture. The apostle Paul writes about the power of love.

Love is patient, love is kind. It does not envy, it does not boast, it is not proud. It is not rude, it is not self-seeking, it is not easily angered, it keeps no record of wrongs. Love does not delight in evil but rejoices with the truth. It always protects, always trusts, always hopes, always perseveres. Love never fails. (1 Cor 13:4-8)

I love my nine-year-old son dearly. He's a great kid. But I have confessed to Jorie and to him that I get frustrated when I ask him to do something and he doesn't do it or gets mad.

He has a great relationship with Jorie. When he comes in the house, he usually makes a beeline to his mom to tell her all about his day. He'll do anything for her. There's hardly ever a time when she can't get him to do something. He brings her breakfast in bed. He puts his arm around her when he sits next to her in church. I asked Jorie recently, "What's the difference between my relationship with him and yours? We both spend lots of time with him. He does just about everything you ask him, but I have a tough time getting him to do anything."

She thought for a while and then replied, "He responds to love. He doesn't like directives or commands very well. He doesn't like being told what to do. But when you love him, he'll do anything to please you. He'll take the initiative in doing things he knows you like." We all respond better to love than to demands.

Jesus teaches us about love in the Sermon on the Mount.

So in everything, do to others what you would have them do to you, for this sums up the Law and the Prophets. . . . But I tell you: Love your enemies and pray for those who persecute you. . . . If you love those who love you, what reward will you get? Are not even the tax collectors doing that? And if you greet only your brothers, what are you doing more than others? Do not even pagans do that? Be perfect, therefore, as your heavenly Father is perfect. (Mt 7:12; 5:44, 46-48) You say, "If you knew the way my in-laws treat me, you'd know what a tall order it is to love them."

Focus on verses 46-48 again. If we think we don't have to love our in-laws because of the way they treat us, we're living by the wrong standard. We're not called to love only those who treat us well. Anybody can fill that order. Jesus Christ is our standard. We are to be perfect as he is perfect.

If you're struggling in your relationship with your in-laws and would like to see things improve, Christ challenges you to make a new resolve to love them. They don't have to do anything to deserve your change in behavior. Simply make a decision, out of obedience to Christ, to love them to the best of your ability. And when your love runs short, ask Christ to fill you with his love.

Love Drives Out Fear

One of the most formidable foes of love is fear. Think for a moment about the kinds of fears you may experience in in-law relationships. Mothers-in-law may fear the relationship itself—not wanting to become the proverbial mother-in-law who is the butt of jokes and criticism. A mother may fear that she is going to be replaced in her son's affection by her daughter-in-law. A mother can also fear losing her daughter to a son-in-law. She can never quite imagine her daughter being as close with a husband as she has been with her mother, and surely no son-in-law could take as good care of her daughter as she did. I suppose that's why they say, "Behind every successful man stands a surprised mother-in-law."

A father, too, may fear his daughter won't be protected sufficiently by the young son-in-law. Along with his wife, a dad can get caught up in the fear that the son- or daughter-in-law is going to take his son or daughter away from him. He may not see his child as much as he did before or talk as frequently. Consequently, he may fear not being as close as before. He may not like the prospect of being supplanted or losing control to someone else.

So a father may try to prove that he is still as close to his child as he always was. He may try to demonstrate that he still holds the top spot in his child's affections. The real problem is that fear of losing a child to the intruding son- or daughter-in-law causes him to withhold love from this new family member. Because parents want so much to keep their children close, they may consciously or unconsciously withhold love from the child's spouse.

Parents may also fear that their child may become closer to the in-law's family than to their own family. This fear may cause them to make derogatory comments about the other parents.

A daughter-in-law may fear she can never be the hostess, decorator or entertainer her mother-in-law is. She may fear that she is not going to be loved as a member of the family. A daughter-in-law who feels hurt over and over again by her parents-in-law may pull away out of fear of further injury. She solves the problem by establishing a pattern of minimal contact. She thinks the solution is avoidance, but she eventually discovers that's no solution.

A son-in-law may fear that his mother-in-law will interfere in his marriage or that he will be disapproved of if he doesn't make as much money as his father-in-law. He may fear that his wife loves her parents more than she loves him.

When Jorie and I married, I had some fears that Jorie would not love me as much as she loved her parents. I knew she was very close to her family. When I heard her talking on the phone to her mother and father, I sensed a tenderness toward them that I was not certain was present in our own relationship. This fear caused me to begin criticizing them in hopes that it would cause Jorie to love me more than them. Naturally, this irrational strategy was doomed to fail. My fear of not being loved by Jorie led me to withhold love from her parents, and that hurt my relationship with them. Thankfully I realized my mistake and took steps to rectify it.

Fear can cause us to keep our in-laws at arm's length. We may exclude them or ignore them at family gatherings. We may treat them like intruders rather than family members. Fear hurts relationships because it translates into *lack of love*.

How do we overcome this fear? The God who made us and created families knows the way. Speaking through John, he says,

There is no fear in love. But perfect love drives out fear, because fear has to do with punishment. The one who fears is not made perfect in love. (1 Jn 4:18)

From the beginning of time, *love* has been God's prescribed solution for the problem of fear. How can we decrease tensions with our in-laws? We must choose to love them by a conscious act of a mature will. We can't overcome fear with fear, jealousy, envy or control. We overcome it with love. We can make a conscious decision that no matter what happens, we're going to love our in-laws.

Jesus said the greatest commandment is to "love the Lord your God with all your heart and with all your soul and with all your mind and with all your strength. The second is this: 'Love your neighbor as yourself' " (Mk 12:29-30). These two commands cover all our relationships, including those with our in-laws. Love is God's prescribed remedy for healing all ties. Are you having a problem with an in-law? Don't reject him. Don't resent her. Don't gossip about him. Don't criticize her. Instead, learn to love him or her. That's God's way. It's easy to say, but not always easy to do.

We hear the cry of the person who says, "Asking me to love my in-laws is really difficult." What about the mother-in-law who never includes her daughter-in-law's name on the letter she writes to her son? How about the parents-in-law who express their disapproval regarding the adoption of a child by refusing to acknowledge the baby's presence, acting as though she doesn't exist? Or the daughter-in-law who refuses to spend any holidays with her husband's family, preferring the traditions of her own family? Or the father-in-law who demands his grandson be given his family name? Are there any suggestions for loving these people? We have two: adopt them into your family and look for ways to help them.

Principle One: Adopt Your In-Laws into Your Family

We are far more likely to experience strong, healthy relationships with our in-laws if we mentally adopt our in-laws as our own family members. Rather than excluding them, treat them like family. One woman writes:

> The first time I met my husband's parents, they hugged and kissed me and made me feel like I was their daughter. At the party, they introduced me to everyone with great affection. I was amazed that they would treat me immediately as one of the family.
>
> It has been like this for the past twenty-plus years of marriage. Once we were married, my mother-in-law always introduced me as her daughter, whether my husband was near or not. I was her daughter, not daughter-in-law. Because she made me feel so special, I called her "Mom" from the start.

Her mother-in-law opened herself up to her, and she responded in kind.

If you want to show that you really love your in-laws and have adopted them into your family, go for broke and introduce them as family. Certainly "Jane" and "Al" are appropriate, as are "Mrs. T" or "Dad Winters." But there is nothing as refreshing as "Mom" and "Dad." Introduce them as your parents or sons or daughters, not just as your in-laws. It will make them feel more like family and will help you treat them more like family.

When a marriage occurs, if you embrace and love the in-laws as your own family, we can almost guarantee that you will cultivate good relationships. When parents view marriage as the loss of a son or a daughter, it is a threatening experience. But if they view marriage as an opportunity to gain a son or daughter, to adopt a new person into their family, then it can be a plus. Do whatever you must to communicate to your in-laws that in your mind they are family. Don't treat them as outsiders, but treat them as your own kin. A daughter-in-law writes:

I remember when John announced that we were going to be married, I was taken aside by his mom. She wanted me to come upstairs and see John's room and what a mess it contained. She did not want me to enter the marriage not knowing what I was in for! She gave me articles on the phases of marriage and the deep love that comes from a strong, long marriage. She made it clear that I was very important to her and the family and she planned on having a permanent addition to her family.

When she travels, she thinks of me. I have angels from around the world that she has given me. It need not be a special day we are celebrating. She simply surprises me with a gift, always with a lovely note attached telling me that she loves me and that I am her angel.

When I am a mother-in-law I want to be just like her. I keep a list of the wonderful things she does, and doesn't do, so, hopefully, I can be half the mother she has been to me.

What did this woman do that was so special? She adopted her son's wife. From the beginning she treated her like her own daughter, not like an intruder.

Natasha Josefowitz writes this in her poem "The People My Children Married":

> If my son brings breakfast in bed to my daughter-in-law,
> she's a lazy good-for-nothing and he spoils her.
> If my son-in-law brings breakfast in bed to my daughter,
> she deserves it and he's a doll.[1]

There is a natural tendency for all of us to give preferential treatment to our own kin and treat our in-laws as something less than family. We've seen many families that visually illustrate this truth at holidays throughout the year. We know of birth children who receive expensive birthday presents while in-law children receive (perhaps) a card. Out-of-town parents may make special trips to visit their birth children but not take the time even to call children-by-marriage on the telephone to wish them a special day.

What does this differentiation communicate? That parents don't love their children by marriage the same as the children they birthed. What's their rationale? "They're not my flesh and blood!" Are they right in perpetuating the distinction? Not if they want a relationship anchored in God's principles. Scripture tells us, "There is neither Jew nor Greek, slave nor free, male nor female, for you are all one in Christ Jesus" (Gal 3:28). God does away with distinctions in his family. He most certainly wants us to do the same.

Lest we get smug, children are guilty too. Often a wife will say, "Honey, you buy your mom's birthday present and card. She's *your* mom!" Emphasizing the distinction between *your* set of parents and *my* set of parents perpetuates divisive thinking. Married children have the unique privilege of having two moms and two dads, and God's best would be to graft them all in as family, without distinction.

Preferential treatment has to go if we want to overcome the traditional difficulties with in-laws. It's a matter of attitude. Do you treat your in-laws as your parents or as outsiders?

We wonder if people who have adopted children might have an advantage in this process. Jorie and I have four boys by biological birth. By the time we birthed our fourth little boy, who looked just like his three older brothers, we realized we had a little-boy mold. We were sure that if we birthed ten children they'd all be boys who looked just alike. Since it appeared that we only had the capacity to birth little boys, we turned to adoption to have a little girl.

In our first adoption, we did not specify whether we wanted a boy or a girl. We loved all our boys, so were happy to adopt a boy or a girl. Somehow, however, I think we assumed that God would bring us a little girl. When the social worker called from the hospital to tell us that our baby had been born, she added, "It's a boy!" We weren't prepared for the emotions that filled our home. Jorie instantly burst into tears. It wasn't that we weren't excited about our little baby boy, but we had assumed God would grant us a girl.

That unmet desire to parent a little girl led us to adopt once again. This time our search led us to the country of Romania. We discovered beautiful two-month-old Andrea lying in a paint-peeled crib, and we rejoiced when the bureaucratic red tape of international adoption was completed and we were able to bring her home to our family.

And, as this book is about to go to the printer, Jorie has just returned from a visit to Vietnam carrying six-week-old Cam Noelle, so we now have two little girls to complement our tribe of five boys.

Do we love all of our children? You bet we do! Our adopted children are just as precious to us as our biological children. Although none of our children have married yet, we suspect that adopting a son- or daughter-in-law and making him or her as special as our own children will be less difficult because we have already had the experience of adopting outsiders into our family. It's a new challenge we look forward to. If you distinguish between your own child and your son- or daughter-in-law, it is unlikely you will discover the closeness Ruth and Naomi found. If you love your sons- or daughters-in-law or mother- or father-in-law and treat them with sensitivity, you will cultivate in-laws who adore you.

In her book *The Friendships of Women,* Dee Brestin tells of the fine experience her sister had with her mother-in-law, Lillian. She didn't realize how much Lillian meant to her sister until after Lillian's death. Her sister was always energetic and seldom heavy-hearted, but in the year following Lillian's death, she was devastated. Seven years later, as the sisters sat together on the beach, Dee asked her why she loved Lillian so much. The words tumbled out, and even then, after so much time, tears welled up in her normally unemotional sister:

Everybody loved Lillian! Just being near her was a comfort and a lift. Her humor, her joy in life, her attentiveness to your thoughts and feelings, her quiet faith. Lillian spent three months living with us one time. My friends raised their eyebrows and said, "Three months? Three months with your mother-in-law in the same house?" But it wasn't a difficult time. It is a joyous, precious memory in our lives.

It helped that she was sensitive to both my need for privacy and my need for help. She would take long walks. She would completely stay out of the kitchen during preparation time. She said two cooks was one too many—so instead she would talk to the kids. I liked that. Then, afterward, she would insist on cleaning up by herself. But I think I was drawn to her because of the way she loved me. I didn't feel like a daughter-in-law but like a beloved daughter. Her actions, her eyes, and her smile told me—but if I didn't know, she wasn't hesitant to express it. If she sensed I was troubled she would say, "I hope you know how very much I love you." . . . I miss her so.[2]

Did you notice that she "didn't feel like a daughter-in-law but like a beloved daughter"? That's the key. Adopt them as your own. Really love them. Most people will respond in kind.

How can parents show they have really adopted their sons- or daughters-in-law? There are many ways, and it only takes some sensitive creativity to begin the process. Keep in mind that often the little things are the most noticed. When writing checks or letters, always include your son- or daughter-in-law's name on them. When you call, always ask about your son- or daughter-in-law, or even better, talk to him or her. Keeping in touch with your son- or daughter-in-law's parents is a thoughtful way to show that you care.

How can sons- or daughters-in-law show they have adopted their mothers- and fathers-in-law as family? Drop your parents-in-law an occasional card thanking them for their role in your mate's life or for allowing you to visit. Call them on the phone every once in a while just like you might call your own parents. Introduce them as "Mom" and "Dad."

Courtesy and respect bring joy to our parents- and children-in-law. One woman writes to her mother-in-law:

You have given me such a wonderful gift to allow your firstborn son to marry me. It has been one of the kindest things you have done for me. I hope our relationship will remain in Christ's love and that we can learn to respect one another more deeply.

Another daughter-in-law writes:

Bob and I were really young when we got married. I was totally accepted and loved as part of the Jones family. In fact, I felt I had more rights than Bob. No matter what my in-laws had to do, they always had time and energy left for me. My mother- and father-in-law's gift to their children and grandchildren, and especially to their daughters-in-law, was unconditional love and kindness.

That's the key. Love.

A mother- and father-in-law wrote the following note to their son-in-law:

37

Dear Son-in-law,

A giant among kings!

These are words we use very lovingly to describe you, Bill. You are such a devoted and loving husband to our dear Peggy and you extend that same devotion and love and teach the value of good morals to our precious grandchildren. Through your devotion and love to your family, your love of Christ has mirrored into our lives and you have added a new and stronger faith within our lives.

We thank God and we thank you, Bill, for being part of our family. Thank you for being "a tower of strength," a "son-in-love" who has added a new dimension to our lives. We love you, Bill!

Mom and Dad

Obviously, Bill is included as one of their family.

When we got married, Jorie's mom sat her down and said, "Now, you make sure you call Ron's mother 'Mom.' "

Jorie said, "Oh, I don't think I can do that. *You're* my mom."

Her mom replied, "Oh yes you can. You just do it."

That was particularly helpful to Jorie. One of the reasons Jorie was afraid to call her mother-in-law "Mom" was that she thought it might hurt her own mom. But when her own mom told her to do it, it freed her up to embrace her mother-in-law like her own mom.

Jorie's parents also reach out to me. Her mom includes my name on letters and packages she sends to Jorie. If a box includes a gift for Jorie, there is always something for me in there as well. I know; I always dig through the box until I find it! Sometimes she surprises me with books or articles she thinks I can use in my preaching and teaching. Sometimes it's food. She figured out that food was the key to her son-in-law's heart. She knows I love pecans, so frequently she will include a batch of freshly baked buttered pecans, just for me. She lets me know she loves me like her own son.

Basically, our relationships boil down to a question of attitude. Do you really want your in-laws to feel a part of your family? Then look for ways to include them and show them unconditional acceptance. Sometimes it's the little things we do that break the ice.

One woman writes:

When Dave and I were first married, I went through the frosted-hair stage. After my trip to the hair salon, other people in my life wasted no time telling me how bad I looked—but not my mother-in-law. I appreciated her silent support.

It's sad to say, but a relationship can be damaged over something as superficial as a hairstyle or the way someone dresses. I know one in-law relationship that was shipwrecked because the daughter-in-law's kitchen wasn't clean enough to eat off the floor.[3]

Nothing will destroy the feeling of family closeness faster than criticism.

Can you have a good relationship with your in-laws? Of course you can. Your in-laws can become some of your finest friends.

Recently we spoke to a man who shared the eulogy at his mother-in-law's funeral. In all the funeral services we have conducted at our church, seldom have in-laws been asked to share eulogies at the memorial service. That the family would ask him testifies of the love he extended to his mother-in-law. Here is a small sampling of what he said about her:

Rachel was so nurturing and caring to everyone she came into contact with. She had a real sweetness about her; she never lost that.

Sometimes I would take Rachel for drives. She was like a child seeing things for the first time. She kept going on and on about how beautiful the clouds were. At the time, I was tired of hearing about clouds, but now I kind of miss it.

In the last year of her life, Rachel referred to me and introduced me as her best friend. Alzheimer's disease was confusing our relationship. I was honored to have been elevated from son-in-law to best friend.

Rachel, I love you and I miss you.

Would that all sons-in-law would love as this man did. May his tribe increase. A conscious choice of our wills to love the in-laws (flaws and all) breaks down our fears. It's a risk worth taking, one gesture at a time.

Look for Ways to Help

Another way we can love our in-laws is by *looking for ways to help them.* This is not a matter of how we feel about them; it is love in action. Jesus teaches us in the Sermon on the Mount, "In everything, do to others what you would have them do to you, for this sums up the Law and the Prophets" (Mt 7:12). All of us know how we like to be treated by others and ways we can use their help. Jesus tells us to look for ways we can do things for others that we ourselves would appreciate.

Parents can strengthen their relationships with their sons- and daughters-in-law by looking for ways they can help their children's marriages. Are there ways to help without interfering? Consider this account told by one young wife:

A Valentine's Day plant arrived for me with a card signed, "From your love," and I assumed it was a gift from my ordinarily inattentive husband. When I thanked him, however, he denied he'd sent it, and over the next few weeks his curiosity about the source of the gift grew into a new tenderness toward me.

I had no idea where the plant had come from and even checked with the florist to make sure it hadn't been a mistake.

"How's the plant?" my mother-in-law asked when she came for a visit about a month later. "The last time I visited," she explained, "you hinted that my son wasn't very attentive. I thought the plant might work. It did twenty years ago when my mother-in-law tried it."[4]

Parents can endear themselves to their sons- and daughters-in-law by making the most of their opportunities to help out in times of stress. When we moved into our newly built home two weeks before Christmas, we foolishly scheduled several parties and open houses at our home within those first weeks. It was a mistake. We had a horrendous amount of work to do. Sensing the stress our party plans had put us under, Ron's mom came down for a few days to help unpack boxes. Jorie greatly appreciated all she did.

One man wrote this to his mother- and father-in law:

Dear Mom,

The kindest thing you have ever done for me is to always be available to help. There are so many little tasks you always seem to have time to do, from ironing my shirt when I am running late to preparing meals for the family. The feeling that you are dependable and can be relied upon is very comforting.

Dear Dad,

The most helpful thing you have ever done for me is to work several days in a row digging and landscaping our yard. You invested so much of your time and really made our home look much better.

I'm not real handy around the house. At least that's the excuse I give Jorie for why I seldom fix things. As a result, Jorie really appreciates it when my dad helps fix things around our house.

Still another way parents can help is by offering to sit with the grandchildren. Every child needs grandparents, and parents can certainly use the help. Offering to baby-sit when you think your adult children could use a break and to step in when one of them is ill is one of the finest ways to express your love.

41

One of the ways Jorie's and my parents have built their relationship with us is by offering to take our kids so that Jorie and I can go out on a date or go for a walk. And my parents have hosted our kids numerous times when one or more of our boys has come their way for a tennis tournament or swim meet. Their willingness to help has freed us from having to travel with our boys numerous times when they have been entered in a weekend sporting event.

When we have gone away on trips, my parents have sometimes come down to take care of our kids. That's a huge gift to us. There are not too many people willing to move in and take care of our tribe! In fact, several years ago, Jorie and I returned from a trip in which my parents were staying with our kids and learned my father had suffered a heart attack! Fortunately, he came through it just fine. The stress that baby-sitting can cause underscores all the more what a gift it is when grandparents offer to take care of grandkids.

One woman wrote the following to her mother-in-law:

Dear Mom,

I appreciate so much that you have always been available to help with our children. When they were young, you were always there to baby-sit when we needed you. And when I was overwhelmed, you were there with your patience, understanding and years of experience.

Another woman writes:

We stayed with my mother- and father-in-law for six weeks after our twins were born. Here we were with a two-year-old, two five-day-old babies, Mark and I, and Dad and Mom. I remember those 2 a.m. feedings. One baby would wake up, and, sure enough, the other one would awake within a few minutes. Mom would always get up to help. She and I would sit in the front room, really tired, but they are great memories, for we would talk and share and laugh.

A helpful mother-in-law established an enduring relationship. Sons- and daughters-in-law can build their relationships with their in-laws by looking for ways to help them too. When we get married, we are no longer under our parents' authority, but we are still to honor our parents. We can honor them by looking for ways to serve them.

Take the Initiative
It's easy to expect our parents to initiate activities with us. That's the role they've always played. We've grown up responding to them. So we wait for them to take the initiative. But now they could be waiting for us to reach out to them. So let's invite them to do some favorite activity or attend a mutually enjoyable event together. If you and your father-in-law enjoy golf, go golfing together. If it's tennis, get on the courts. If you and your mother-in-law enjoy shopping, take her to the mall. If she enjoys walking, join her for a walk. Or what they would really like may be some help with projects around their house. You'll be amazed how simple things like these can open the doors to a deeper relationship.

There are other ways to show thoughtfulness. You can write to your in-laws. In our computer age a handwritten note can mean a lot to a parent. If you want to go high-tech, communicate through e-mail. Thank your in-laws for the wonderful job they did raising your mate. Several times I have written my mother- and father-in-law to thank them for the qualities of cheerfulness, creativity, ingenuity and perseverance they helped build into Jorie. Each time they have been delighted with my notes.

Daughters-in-law can improve their relationship with their mothers-in-law by communicating with them frequently. The mother-in-law/daughter-in-law relationship is often the most difficult one to cultivate. One of the reasons a woman feels more anxiety about letting a son go than a daughter is that the son is less apt to keep close contact. There's some sad truth in the old saying, "A son is a son 'til he takes a wife, but a daughter's a daughter the rest of her life." Because many women have a gift for nurturing relationships, they're less likely to emotionally abandon their parents; they're more faithful in writing, calling, visiting and expressing affection.

A daughter-in-law who recognizes this tendency for her husband to not stay in close contact with his parents can show love to her in-laws and improve her relationship with them by taking time to communicate with them. Keeping the mother-in-law informed will do wonders for their relationship and help the mother-in-law not feel that she has lost a son but, rather, that she has gained a daughter.

A member of our church passed on to me a poem given to her by an elderly friend who had received it from one of her grateful daughters-in-law.

To His Mother
"Mother-in-law," they say, and yet
Somehow I simply can't forget
'twas you who watched his baby ways,
Who taught him his first hymn of praise,
Who smiled on him with loving pride
When he first toddled by your side.
"Mother-in-law"—but oh, 'twas you
Who taught him to be kind and true.
When he was tired, almost asleep,
'twas to your arms he used to creep.
And when he bruised his tiny knee,
'twas you who kissed it tenderly.
"Mother-in-law," they say, and yet
Somehow I never shall forget
How very much I owe

To you, who taught him how to grow.
You trained your son to look above,
You made of him the man I love.
And so I think of that today—
Ah, then with thankful heart I'll say,
"Our mother!"[5]

Including in-laws in special celebrations is another way to show thoughtfulness. With seven children, we have a lot of special celebrations—birthdays, baptisms, soccer or basketball championships, tennis-tournament victories, dramas, musical performances and graduations. Although neither set of grandparents lives in town with us, we've tried to include them in these special occasions.

The health of our relationships with our in-laws is largely a matter of our attitude. We can't do much about what our in-laws think of us or about the way they treat us, but we can do something about how we think of them and how we treat them. If we love them, more than likely they will love us (if not at present, they will gradually come to respond to our initiative of love). If we respect them, there's a high chance they'll respect us. If we trust them and think well of them, more than likely they will think kindly of us.

We challenge you to love your in-laws like never before. If for no other reason, do it as a measure of your love for Christ. The apostle John writes:

> If anyone says, "I love God," yet hates his brother, he is a liar. For anyone who does not love his brother, whom he has seen, cannot love God, whom he has not seen. And he has given us this command: Whoever loves God must also love his brother. (1 Jn 4:20-21)

If you are unable to love your in-laws, Scripture says it calls into question your love for God. So if for no other reason, why don't you begin to love them as an expression of your love for God?

Wouldn't it be fun to be referred to as an angel or best friend by your in-laws? It can happen. It starts with one person taking the risk to love. Are you willing to be the one who takes the initiative, to begin to love them as Christ loves you?

Questions for Reflection or Discussion:

1. Read Ruth 1—2. Note all the statements and actions of Ruth's mother-in-law. What did she say or do that made her a great mother-in-law?

2. Read 1 John 4:18. Why does perfect love drive out fear? Describe how you think love casts aside fear.

3. Read 1 Corinthians 13:1-8. Read it again, replacing the word *love* with your name. How would loving like this help your relationship with your in-laws?

4. How can "adopting" your in-laws as part of your own family help you better love your in-laws?

5. How does looking for ways to help your in-laws help you show that you love them? What are some ways you have helped your in-laws, and how have those actions affected your relationship with them?

6. What principle or insight in this chapter was most helpful to you?

3
Healthy Self-Esteem: A Necessity for Love

E *very time my husband's parents* leave I cry for days," the young wife shared, reddened eyes brimming. "I spend days before they come anticipating their arrival. I clean my house, prepare the best meals I can fix and dress the kids in their cutest clothes, in hopes that this time they'll notice and be pleased.

"But nothing ever changes. Though I straighten the house after everyone's in bed, get up early to prepare special 'company' breakfasts and try to make sure the children are well-behaved, I never receive a compliment. They notice only the things that are wrong. This time, after a whole weekend of trying to please them, all they said was, 'The kids are too noisy at meals.' Why don't they like me? I feel so worthless when I'm with them."

This young wife expresses the sentiments of thousands of in-laws around the world. Many married people and parents of married children suffer from feelings of insecurity, insignificance, worthlessness or inferiority—and, obviously, these feelings affect in-law relationships. This is where our second principle comes from.

Principle Two: Love for In-Laws Emanates from Healthy Self-Esteem

Healthy self-esteem is far more important to strong relationships with in-laws than most people realize. People with low self-esteem experience insecurity, so they are far less likely to express the love that is essential to good relationships with in-laws. In contrast, people with high self-esteem are less likely to be threatened by in-laws or foster feelings of envy, jealousy and mistrust—the enemies of good relationships. Healthy self-esteem enables us to be gracious toward our in-laws and give them the affirmation they crave. When we compliment and appreciate our in-laws, they are far more willing to extend kindness in return.

If you struggle with feelings of low self-esteem, this may explain why you have a hard time loving your in-laws and why you may feel they are unkind to you. If your in-laws suffer from a poor self-image, this could explain why they are threatened by you and treat you less than kindly. Since healthy self-esteem is the reservoir from which love emanates, it is a significant factor in improving relationships with in-laws.

How does the Christian faith make a difference in how we feel about ourselves? Paul tells us, "If anyone is in Christ, he is a new creation; the old has gone, the new has come!" (2 Cor 5:17). When a person accepts Christ, a process of transformation is set in motion. Each of us remains a frail human being but has a new, perfect identity given to us at our conversion. Our self-esteem and subsequent actions will be affected by how we view this transformation that has already taken place.

Unfortunately, feelings of inadequacy can and do linger, because the factors that influenced the formation of our self-image do not change. Because we cannot undo our childhood experiences or change the hurtful incidents in our past, our self-image can be very resistant to the gospel's transforming power.

You may be a believer who struggles with self-worth due to factors from your past that haunt you and make you feel inadequate. Or you may recently have been leveled by hurtful comments or actions from your in-laws. Deep down inside, their attitudes have shaken your confidence in yourself. You may even be wondering why God put you on this earth. But if you don't face and deal with your shaken self-concept, it will adversely affect your relationships with your in-laws and with others.

What Is Self-Esteem?

Simply stated, self-esteem is the picture of ourselves that we carry at the center of our heart.

Have you ever shown someone the pictures in your wallet? You were probably inwardly pleased when the person liked the photo of someone really special to you—your boyfriend or girlfriend, your beautiful children. But how did you feel when your friend saw the picture on your driver's license? Few people are pleased with their photo taken at the Department of Motor Vehicles.

The last picture Jorie had taken for her driver's license was a disaster. She had two toddlers pulling at her legs and was holding our two-month-old baby boy. Just at the moment of the click, one of the boys asked her a question, causing her to lean down sideways so she could hear him better. The clicking shutter preserved my harried wife for eight years. Her crooked mouth and downturned eyes made her declare she looked like she'd had a stroke! And after four years of showing it on demand for identification, she was further punished by a perfect driving record that offered her a four-year extension of that driver's license. When it finally expired, she was determined not to live another eight years in humiliation. She left all the kids home and spent extra time on her hair before going to get her new picture taken!

But our driver's license photo is only one of the many pictures of ourselves we carry around. Each of us carries another portrait with us, a picture far more important than any in our wallet. Psychologists have a name for it. They call this mental picture of ourselves our *self-image.* Whether we call it self-concept, self-worth or self-esteem, we're talking about the way we feel about ourselves. It isn't so much who we are but who we *think* we are that determines our responses to situations.

In *The Magic Power of Self-Image Psychology,* Maxwell Maltz writes:
The discovery of the self-image is one of the most important finds of this century. For, though we may not realize it, we all do carry with us this mental blueprint or picture of ourselves. . . . Furthermore, all our actions and emotions are consistent with our self-image. You will act like the sort of person you think you are.[1]

John Devines, author of *How Much Are You Worth?* summarizes the importance of self-esteem. Your view of yourself, he writes, is "far more important than most people think." He says,

The answer to how much I am worth determines
whether I am happy or sad,
excited or depressed,
in love with life
or thinking about suicide.

If I think that I am valuable—worth a lot—
I will function well at my job,

get along better with my spouse,
and have a tremendous sense of well-being.
But if I think I am worthless,
I lack motivation for work,
and am convinced that everything I do will fail.[2]

Whether we like it or not, our mental self-portrait has a tremendous bearing on our emotional and spiritual well-being and on all our relationships. Research has shown that we tend to act in harmony with our mental self-portrait. If we don't like the kind of person we are, we think no one else likes us either. And that influences our social life, our job performance and our relationships with others—including, naturally, our in-laws. A healthy self-concept is a precious possession. An inadequate self-concept is a handicap. If we are seeking to improve our relationship with our in-laws, we must evaluate our own self-esteem.

What Are Some Indicators of Low Self-Esteem?

Before going further, it may be helpful to do some self-analysis to ascertain whether you or your in-laws may suffer from low self-esteem. Listed below are some common indicators of low self-esteem. Ask yourself if these statements are true of you or of one of your in-laws:

☐ pessimistic outlook on life
☐ lack of confidence in social skills
☐ extreme sensitivity to the opinions of other people
☐ intensely self-conscious about appearance, performance or status
☐ competitive view toward others
☐ striving to become something or someone different instead of relaxing and enjoying one's own uniqueness
☐ problem with believing or accepting God's love or the love of another person

☐ defensive in behavior and conversations

☐ carrying a chip on their shoulder, being highly critical of others and unable to compliment others

☐ tendency to develop clinging relationships

☐ inability to accept or give praise

☐ habit of letting others "walk" on them

☐ dependence on material possessions for security

☐ habitually using negative labels when referring to themselves and others

☐ tendency to follow the crowd and avoid independent behavior

☐ difficulty in establishing close relationships; focus on meeting their own needs rather than meeting the needs of others

☐ need to control others[3]

Because people with low self-esteem spend so much time seeking to meet their own needs, they have little time left to meet the needs of others. So it should not surprise us that people with poor self-images have difficulty getting along with their in-laws. They are so insecure and self-absorbed in their own inadequacies that they have little energy left to reach out in love to their in-laws.

What Factors Shape Our Self-Esteem?

Three basic emotional needs are common to all people:

1. The need to feel loved and have a sense of belonging

2. The need to feel acceptable and have a sense of worthiness

3. The need to feel adequate and have a sense of competence

These serve as three pillars around which our self-image is developed. Belonging, worthiness, and competence are the supports on which a healthy self-image rests.[4]

The first pillar is *the need to feel loved and have a sense of belonging.* Research has demonstrated that the single most important factor in developing a healthy personality is the sense of being loved. The initial development of our self-image comes from our relationships with our parents. Children learn what kind of people they are and how they should feel about themselves by the reactions of their parents to them. A child who is repeatedly called bad, lazy, no good, stupid, shy or clumsy will tend to act out this picture which the parent or authority figure has created.

During my senior year in college, I took a trip around the world. I stayed with a college buddy, Andy, and his family in Hong Kong for ten days.

Andy's younger brother, Tom, was short and stocky, built in the shape of a ball. He suffered from epilepsy. He kept a lemon by his pillow at night and in his pocket during the day. If he had an epileptic attack, inhaling the lemon scent would stabilize him.

One night Andy and I were going out with a couple of girls. I said to Tom, who was watching me shave, "Why don't you come along?"

"Why do you want me?" he responded with a surprised look. "I'm fat and have to carry around this stupid lemon. Nobody likes me." He could not fathom anyone really caring about him and wanting to include him.

I encouraged him to come. He did—and had a great time. He longed to be loved.

Although adults may be more sophisticated than children, they still have a need to feel loved and to belong. Most engaged couples looking forward to marriage long to be loved by their new parents-in-law and long to feel that they belong in their new family. Most parents of a bridal couple look forward to gaining a new child and becoming a revered new parent. But reality tells us this basic longing often doesn't get met. Too many in-law relationships—even in Christian families—are tense and painfully strained because the in-laws do not give each other the love and sense of belonging they need. If you see your mate struggling with his or her relationship with in-laws, one of the things you can do to help is work to love your spouse and help strengthen his or her self-esteem.

Closely related to the need to feel loved is the second pillar: *the need to feel acceptable and have a sense of worthiness.* Belonging is the sense of being loved by others. Related to it is a sense of worthiness, a feeling of being acceptable to yourself and accepted by others. If you are accepted by others, you will more likely feel acceptable to yourself. Andy's brother Tom felt unacceptable because of his looks and his physical challenge; when we included him that evening, he felt accepted—and therefore worth something.

In a healthy in-law relationship, people are cherished and continually made to feel accepted and worthy. In a painfully strained in-law relationship, people suffer from feelings of rejection and are made to feel worthless.

One of the ways we assess our personal worth is by examining our physical appearance. When it comes to beauty, almost all of us suffer from feelings of inadequacy. *Leadership* reported that 99 percent of women would change something about their looks if they could, and 94 percent of men would.[5] If feelings of physical inadequacy cause us to feel unworthy, we will live each day in fear of rejection. Wise in-laws understand that most people harbor some feelings of physical inadequacy, so they are careful never to say anything that might be construed as a criticism of an in-law's physical appearance. Being quick to affirm your mate's appearance and being liberal with praise toward his or her achievements may bolster your mate's self-confidence and translate into a better relationship with in-laws as well.

The third pillar from which we formulate our self-esteem is *the need to feel adequate and have a sense of competence.* In this case we ask ourselves, "How am I doing?" or "How am I doing in comparison with others?" Psychologists tell us that the rudiments of self-concept are formed by childhood family and school experiences, when we first test our academic and athletic skills. By the age of five or six, our self-concept—the person we think we are in relationship to others—is so firmly established that we will resist efforts to change it.

The American Institute of Family Relations reported a survey in which parents were asked to record how many negative—as opposed to positive—comments they made to their children. The results showed that they criticized ten times for every favorable comment. In a survey in Orlando, Florida, teachers were found to be 75 percent negative. And it was learned that it takes four positive statements from a teacher to offset the effects of one negative statement to a child.[6]

This means that most of us, as we approach marriage and in-law relationships, have fragile self-concepts. We enter marriage with a desire to feel adequate and competent. A new bride and groom are taking on new responsibilities and are anxious to demonstrate to each other and to their respective families their competence in these new roles. New parents-in-law are moving from a comfortable, established role as parents to a new role as in-laws. All these individuals have the need to feel competent and adequate in their new positions. If our self-esteem is shaky, it's no wonder many of us struggle with these tricky yet vitally important relationships with in-laws.

At this point you may be thinking, "No wonder I suffer from feelings of inadequacy with my in-laws and have such a tough time handling hurtful comments from them. It looks like I got a bad foundation! Is it possible to re-lay a foundation that was so poorly laid?"

Yes. The good news is that your self-portrait is not permanently affixed like a photo I.D. in your wallet. With God's help, you can change your self-esteem and salvage your in-law relationships. God can help you cultivate a healthy self-esteem by enabling you to see yourself as he sees you. In the process, he meets all three of your most important emotional needs.

We want to offer six suggestions for improving your self-esteem and the self-esteem of your in-laws, giving you a chance to have the rich relationship with your in-laws that God intended you to have.

1. Our need for belonging rests on God the Father. God says,

Let us make man in our image, in our likeness, and let them rule over the fish of the sea and the birds of the air, over the livestock, over all the earth, and over all the creatures that move along the ground. (Gen 1:26)

The psalmist writes:

What is man that you are mindful of him, the son of man that you care for him? You made him a little lower than the heavenly beings and crowned him with glory and honor. You made him ruler over the works of your hands; you put everything under his feet. (Ps 8:4-6)

Our worth is forever established by the fact that we were created in God's image. Christianity declares all-out war on the destructive value system in which we live, a system which reserves self-worth for a select minority. By his creation, God proclaims that all human beings are infinitely valuable because they were created in the image of God.

When we look at God's creation, we are awestruck by the beauty of the mountains, the rivers, the sun and the moon. Yet how can we praise the beauty of a sunset or a flower and at the same time downgrade ourselves? Is not the human being the most marvelous creation of all? The psalmist says that we are the apex of God's creation.

The psalmist writes further:

For you created my inmost being;

you knit me together in my mother's womb.

I praise you because I am fearfully and wonderfully made;

your works are wonderful, I know that full well (Ps 139:13-14).

Isn't this true? We are a species of wonder. No one would argue that the human body is a phenomenal combination of strength, beauty, coordination, grace and balance.

Jesus speaks of our infinite value:

Are not two sparrows sold for a penny? Yet not one of them will fall to the ground apart from the will of your Father. And even the very hairs of your head are all numbered. So don't be afraid; you are worth more than many sparrows. (Mt 10:29-31)

Christ differentiates between humans and the rest of the animal kingdom. Humankind alone is made in the image of God. Humans differ in kind from all other animals by virtue of their reasoning powers. God cares about all his creation, but humanity is the focus of special attention. Jesus knew that hardships in life could be more successfully handled if one's sense of self-worth was secure. He knew we could be more successful in overcoming feelings of fear and rejection if our self-esteem was established by how God values us.

Yes, it's important for a daughter-in-law to be loved, to feel she is an adored member of the family whose name she has added to her own. But if she knows she belongs to the King of the universe as a treasured member of his family, the need for love and approval from her in-laws pales in comparison. Yes, a mother may fear losing the closeness with her favorite daughter to her new son-in-law, realizing that the marriage relationship must now take precedence over hers. But if that mother's sense of belonging is rooted in her own realization of God's infinite love for her, she isn't threatened by her daughter's new love. Marriage and in-law relationships are important—but not as important as fostering the understanding that our real sense of security comes through our belonging to God.

However, old patterns are hard to change. Circus elephants are a prime example of this fact. Have you ever watched the elephants at a circus? They stand in place with nothing more than an unattached chain dangling around one of their feet. Don't you wonder why they don't wander off into the stands? Who could stop them?

They stay in place because they have a very long memory. When they're babies, the trainers stake them down. They try to tug away from the stake, maybe ten thousand times, before they realize that they can't possibly get away. At that point their "elephant memory" takes over and they remember for the rest of their lives that they can't get away from the stake. Because of that memory, adult elephants can be kept in place by a small stake that could be easily uprooted if the elephant would only try. Eventually, the elephant stays put by nothing more than a chain around its foot, even though it is attached to nothing.

We humans are sometimes like elephants. When we were teenagers we may have heard someone say about us, "He's not very good-looking," or "She's an airhead." And *zap*, it drove a stake into our mind. Years later, we can be ensnared once again by an insulting remark callously made by one of our in-laws.

If we want to be freed from carry-over hurts from our backgrounds and keep from being leveled by derogatory remarks made by an in-law, we must let the truth of our creation in the image of God sink deep into our consciousness. If you struggle with your self-worth, trace your roots in God.

2. Our worthiness rests on God the Son. Our need to feel acceptable and have a sense of worthiness rests on an understanding of the redemption of God the Son. Scripture tells us: "God demonstrates his own love for us in this: While we were still sinners, Christ died for us" (Rom 5:8). And, "This is love: not that we loved God, but that he loved us and sent his Son as an atoning sacrifice for our sins" (1 Jn 4:10).

Christ considered us so worthwhile that he came to die for us. He died in our place because he saw us as people made in God's image.

Our sins were the cause but not the reason he gave his life for us. The reason was that he knew our worth. We are forgiven not because we did anything to deserve it but because we are worth it. If Christ says we are so valuable that we're worth dying for, who can take away our worth? The apostle Paul asks:

What, then, shall we say in response to this? If God is for us, who can be against us? He who did not spare his own Son, but gave him up for us all—how will he not also, along with him, graciously give us all things? Who will bring any charge against those whom God has chosen? It is God who justifies. Who is he that condemns? Christ Jesus, who died—more than that, who was raised to life—is at the right hand of God and is also interceding for us. (Rom 8:31-34)

If Christ says we are of high value, who's going to argue with him?

If comments made by your in-laws cause you to suffer from feelings of worthlessness, flood your mind with the truth that Christ died for you. We believe that if you were the only human on earth, Jesus would have died for you just the same. The cross is the greatest symbol ever of the affirmation of your worth as a human being. It is the divine seal of your human dignity.

A young husband who understands the reality that the God of the universe loved him enough to die for him can be generous to his young wife, realizing she can be friends with her mom without taking away from him. A father can relax if his son-in-law's family pays for trips for his daughter's family to go to Hawaii or helps with a down payment for a house, realizing that his worth comes not from his ability to provide for his family but from his redemption by Christ. Competition and insecurity in in-law relationships can diminish drastically with understanding of our worth in Christ.

3. Our competence rests on God the Spirit. Our need to feel adequate and have a sense of competence rests on the transforming power of God

the Spirit in our lives. When we disobey God and break his command-
ments, we feel guilty. When we lie, steal, lust or hate, we feel crummy
about ourselves. If we violate God's standards, we lose our self-respect
and eventually undermine our self-esteem.

The good news is that we do not have to live in miserable defeat. We
are equipped to obey God by the indwelling power of the Holy Spirit,
who gives us power to overcome our sinful nature. With his divine
power working within us, we can face every situation with confidence.
Our adequacy is not in ourselves but in him. The key lies in allowing
the Holy Spirit to fill or empower us moment by moment. Paul writes,
"Live by the Spirit and you will not gratify the desires of the sinful
nature" (Gal 5:16). The Holy Spirit has the power to help us overcome
the desires of the sinful nature. If we depend on the power of the Spirit
for everything we do, we don't have to live in defeat. Paul writes: "Not
that we are competent in ourselves to claim anything for ourselves, but
our competence comes from God" (2 Cor 3:5). And, "I can do everything through him who gives me strength" (Phil 4:13). When we realize
who we are in Christ, we feel much better about ourselves.

And the Holy Spirit gives us the power to change, so that we do not
need to lash back in anger at in-laws who treat us unfairly. The Holy
Spirit gives us power to love our in-laws even when we do not sense
any love being reciprocated. Our self-images will soar as we begin to
love our in-laws as Christ loves us and respond to them in a way that
is pleasing in the eyes of God.

We know many people who hold deep-seated feelings of bitterness
toward their in-laws. They feel very guilty about the way they feel, but
they do not know how else to respond to the mistreatment they feel
from their in-laws. We believe that rather than berating ourselves for our
negative feelings and for the rotten things we do, we need to start
believing in who we are in Christ and who we can become through the

strength of the Holy Spirit. If we get down on ourselves and believe we will never get better, we reveal a lack of prayer and lack of faith in the power of the Spirit to transform us. If we focus on who we can become in Christ, we are far more likely to become victorious Christians.

One woman confessed that her coping mechanism for surviving times with her husband's family was to make sure she never spoke about herself in her mother-in-law's presence. It was strange: Although the mother-in-law would pleasantly discuss her son and grandchildren, she would never ask even one question concerning her daughter-in-law's health or activities. If the daughter-in-law chose to share any information about herself, the atmosphere became chilly and strained. This daughter-in-law learned that her in-laws did not want to talk about her. At first she found this devastating—her very personhood was ignored. She longed for her in-laws to love her and show an interest in her life, not just her husband and children's. But as she realized that her worth was dependent not on her in-laws' approval but on God's, she became able to participate in family gatherings confident that she was a whole person, with or without their approval. She was not able to change the unhealthy pattern they had established, but she could stay clear of the damage it might have caused.

Understanding the Holy Spirit's power to change lives gives us hope in two ways. One, we know that the Holy Spirit can transform our attitudes toward our in-laws and way we treat them. Two, we recognize that as we pray for our in-laws, the Spirit can change them. If you look only at who your in-laws are right now, you may feel that an improvement in your relationship looks hopeless. But if you recognize who they can become in Christ, the picture changes. As you accept the responsibility to pray for them to become all that God wants them to be, you can look with expectation for the work of the Spirit in their lives.

4. Change what you can and accept what you cannot. Acceptance of the truth that we are created in God's image and wonderfully made does not mean we should never take steps to change things about ourselves. We should change what we can—and accept what we cannot change. You can't change your in-laws, but you can alter a bad attitude you hold toward them or an obnoxious habit that annoys them.

Just as no one should marry expecting to change his or her mate, we do not believe anyone should expect to change the in-laws. Although we can pray for our in-laws and look for God to work in their lives, we think it is healthier to begin with the assumption: "My in-laws are who they are. Now, what can I do to make the best of it?"

Ask the Lord, "God, What do you want to teach me in this relationship? Are there changes in my attitude and behavior that you want to bring about?" Remember that God isn't half as interested in the way your in-laws treat you as he is in your response to them. If he can teach you to love them even when they don't love you, he has brought about growth in you and caused good to come out of a difficult situation.

Since your ability to love your in-laws may be, in part, predicated on how you feel about yourself, there may also be changes that you can make personally that cause you to feel better about yourself. If finishing a college or graduate degree is important to you and would make you feel better about yourself, finish it. If you've allowed yourself to get overweight and feel crummy about your appearance, take steps to shed the pounds. If your teeth are crooked and it is financially possible to do so, have them straightened.

However, some things about our physical appearance and intellectual capacities cannot be changed. We must accept what we cannot change and trust that God did not make a mistake in the way he made us. The apostle Paul writes about his "thorn in the flesh":

Three times I pleaded with the Lord to take it away from me. But he said to me, "My grace is sufficient for you, for my power is made perfect in weakness." Therefore I will boast all the more gladly about my weaknesses, so that Christ's power may rest on me. (2 Cor 12:8-9) He prayed for God to heal him. God did not. Was he angry? No. He thanked God that he could demonstrate God's grace through his weakness. We too should respond to our flaws in this fashion. Even if our in-laws make critical remarks about our appearance or abilities, it need not threaten our self-esteem, because we know God doesn't make junk.

5. *Think and speak positively about yourself and your in-laws.* What we think and speak about ourselves, to a great degree, determines who we are. Positive thinking isn't just brainwashing ourselves; it is bringing the way we view ourselves in line with the way God sees us and refusing to think or say things that tear down our self-images. Thinking positively about ourselves, as God thinks of us, makes an unbelievable difference in the way we view ourselves and has everything to do with the way we act. You were created in God's image, Christ died for you and the Holy Spirit makes you adequate to face any situation. Now live in the light of these truths.

In like fashion, the way we think about our in-laws has a lot to do with the way we treat them.

The apostle Paul tells us how we ought to think:

Finally, brothers, whatever is true, whatever is noble, whatever is right, whatever is pure, whatever is lovely, whatever is admirable— if anything is excellent or praiseworthy—think about such things. (Phil 4:8)

In short, we are to think positive thoughts about our in-laws. It will make a huge difference in the way we treat them.

Goethe said, "If you treat a man as he is, he will stay as he is. But if you treat him as if he were what he ought to be, and could be, he will become that bigger and better man." So let's begin to think positively about our in-laws and express appreciation to them for who they are and encourage them in all that they are capable of becoming. Let's concentrate on strengths and virtues instead of weaknesses and faults. As we expect the best in them, our expectations will become a self-fulfilling prophecy.

6. *Give your in-laws the blessing of affirmation.* Instead of thinking and speaking negatively about our in-laws, we should offer words of affirmation. "When we are cursed, we bless" (1 Cor 4:12). "Bless those who persecute you; bless and do not curse" (Rom 12:14). It is only when we give blessing and affirmation that we are able to foster high self-esteem in people around us.

Ted Miller describes how artist Benjamin West became a painter:

One day his mother went out leaving him in charge of his little sister, Sally. In his mother's absence he discovered some bottles of colored ink and began to paint Sally's portrait. In doing so he splattered ink over the table and floor. When his mother returned she saw the mess but said nothing. She picked up the piece of paper and looked at his drawing. "Why," she said, "it's Sally!" and she stopped and kissed him. West said, "My mother's kiss that day made me a painter."[7]

She loved him unconditionally. Rather than rebuking him for messing up the house, she praised his effort at painting.

We have in our home a special plate that we use to affirm and encourage the members of our family. The plate has four words on it: "You are special today." Not only on birthdays and Father's Day, but whenever someone has made a special achievement or effort, we recognize that by serving his or her meal on the red plate. Each time Jorie delivered a baby, she ate from the red plate when she came home. Our children each were granted the honor of eating from the red plate on the respective days when they were officially potty trained. The day Jorie received her first book contract from a publisher, she sat before the red plate. When one family member is particularly discouraged or sad, the red plate appears. This is one way we affirm one another in our home.

Just as parents who bestow a lot of affirmation on their family members produce children with high self-esteem, relationships with in-laws could be radically improved if we put into practice the biblical principle of affirmation. Rather than affirming, most of us are quick to criticize.

And great harm can result—harm we never would have intended. Whenever Ann and Jed were with Jed's parents, the parents criticized everything both of them did. In contrast, they praised Jed's sister, Ruth, and her husband, Joe, and talked about how great they were in so many ways. This caused unending distress, including some jealousy! Then one day, in conversation with Ruth, Ann found that the parents treated them exactly the same way, always praising Jed and Ann and never having anything nice to say to Ruth or Joe. In discovering this fact, the young couples felt the pressure lift. They came to understand that this was simply their parents' relating pattern—and that in their own warped way they did appreciate all of their children.

Your in-laws may be quick to criticize and slow to affirm. This does not necessarily mean that they do not love you and are not proud of you. We have heard numerous times that both our sets of parents have bragged about us and our children to their friends far more than they have personally complimented us. If we come to realize that we have in-laws who do not give compliments readily, we will no longer be crushed by the lack of affirmation.

More than we like to admit, we are quick to point it out when an in-law makes a mistake. In contrast, when he or she does something well, often little or nothing is said. Yet, our in-law relationships can be devastated by criticism. Wise is the person who understands that self-esteem is the most fragile characteristic in human nature. Once broken, its reconstruction is more difficult than repairing Humpty Dumpty. So, instead of tearing down your in-laws, resolve to offer words of appreciation to them. If you feel you are spoken to rudely, do not respond in kind. Instead, reply with a blessing. That is God's way. Rather than looking for ways to hurt or get back at your in-laws, look for ways to affirm.

Some of the best ways to show affirmation are through significant touches, sincere compliments and reminders of who we are in Christ. How many times have you hugged your daughter-in-law or complimented your mother-in-law? Have you told her how important she is to you lately? Would your son-in-law or father-in-law say you are an affirming person?

Many in-laws feel worthless and unloved in the presence of their children or parents. Yet understanding self-esteem as God intended can help all of us become confident and secure, regardless of which role we fill, because we are of infinite worth to God.

Questions for Reflection or Discussion:

1. "Love emanates from healthy self-esteem." Interact with this statement. Tell why you agree or disagree with the thesis that a healthy view of ourselves is important to learning to love our in-laws.

2. Review the list of indicators of low self-esteem. Which of these indications do you find true of yourself or your in-laws? In what ways have these indicators inhibited love in your relationship with your in-laws?

3. Read Genesis 1:26, Psalm 8:4-6 and Psalm 139:13-14. How does an understanding that God has created us in his own image help us feel good about ourselves and be better able to love our in-laws?

4. Read Romans 5:8, 1 John 4:10 and Romans 8:31-34. How does the death of Christ on our behalf help us with our self-esteem and help us love our in-laws?

5. Read Galatians 5:16, 2 Corinthians 3:5 and Philippians 4:13. How does the power of the Holy Spirit working in us strengthen our self-esteem and encourage us in our duty of love toward our in-laws?

6. Read Philippians 4:8. Why is it important for us to think and speak positively about ourselves?

7. What principle or insight in this chapter was most helpful to you?

4
Leaving
& Cleaving

E *very time I hear the American folk* song "Billy Boy," I smile. Maybe you don't know all the lyrics, so you never discovered why Billy Boy and his girlfriend didn't marry. When you sing, "She's a young thing and cannot leave her mother," you get the impression the girlfriend was twelve or thirteen, or certainly not over fifteen. Wrong! Listen to the stanza:

How old is she, Billy Boy, Billy Boy?
How old is she, charming Billy?
Three times six and four times seven,
Twenty-eight and eleven,
She's a young thing and cannot leave her mother.

Can you believe it? Billy Boy's girlfriend was eighty-five years old! Makes you wonder how old her mother was, doesn't it?

Principle Three: Married Children Must Leave Their Parents and Cleave to Their Spouses

In order for a healthy marriage to be established, married children must make a decisive act of *leaving* the parent-child relationship they formerly maintained and *cleaving* to their new spouse. Shortly after God created Eve and brought her to Adam, he gave them the first marital advice: "For this reason a man will leave his father and mother and be united to his wife, and they will become one flesh" (Gen 2:24). In this sage marriage counsel, God reveals a principle critical for building good relationships with in-laws. When it is violated, it is nearly impossible to establish a good relationship with your in-laws. We've all heard the saying "She's still tied to her mother's apron strings." What is necessary is not just a physical leaving but also a cutting of the umbilical cord of emotional dependence on our parents.

The wise mother- or father-in-law allows, and, if necessary, urges married children to leave so that they might cleave to their mate. Wise children understand that once they are married they must not lean on their moms and dads as they did as children but must establish themselves as a separate and independent family—still related, but now friends. Leaving must occur before a marriage will achieve cleaving. Unless this principle is observed by both children and parents, there is no hope of a healthy in-law relationship.

Leaving Parents

The Hebrew word for *leave* means "abandon" or "break off completely." God calls for the old parent-child relationship to cease. By this God means that in issues of authority the parents no longer have responsibility. A prerequisite for a good marriage is a willingness on the part of the child to leave the parents. Some people are never ready for marriage because they refuse to give up dependence on their parents and make their spouse their number-one priority.

Does leaving mean the parental relationship must end? No, of course not. God calls us to continue to honor our parents (Eph 6:2-3). But without the strong command for men and women to put their full trust in their mates, no marriage would ever experience real success. God knew that after twenty or more years of responding to parental authority, young couples might still depend on their parents even after marriage. Therefore he requires the formal termination of parental authority and a firm commitment to the marriage. Husbands and wives are to make decisions together, independent of parental control.

A practice that enhances the process of leaving, both for parents and children, is the custom of the children asking permission from their parents before announcing an engagement. When couples come to me for marriage, I insist that they both seek their parents' blessing before we proceed with their wedding plans. I believe this crystallizes an important milestone in the relationship. Unfortunately, this propriety is being ignored by many today. I think more young people would return to this observance if they realized how much it can help the process of leaving parents and cleaving to each other.

Look what happened to one young woman:

I requested that Dave speak with my father prior to asking for my hand in marriage. He did so, and my father has remarked about this for years. We broke our engagement the first time (Dave's decision), and when Dave made his final decision, I asked him again to talk with my dad. My father was a bit reticent to agree the second time, but he did, and has continued to comment on Dave's courage in facing him twice! My dad is a very difficult man, and I was the first to marry, so this act by Dave built a bridge between them. I sincerely believe we have peace with my dad because of Dave's going to him first.

When the young man formally asks for the daughter's hand in marriage, it allows her parents to grant permission and give their blessing. It marks the end of their role of authority over their daughter. When the man skips this meaningful step, the parents may feel as if their daughter has been stolen, and that makes it harder for them to release her. For the same reason it is equally important for the couple to seek a blessing from the man's parents.

What does God mean when he says that children must leave their parents and cleave to their mate? In order for cleaving to take place, it seems to us there are several crucial cords to cut in the parent-child relationship.

Financial Dependence

The cord of financial dependence must be cut. Children must make it on their own rather than depend on their parents. If we want to get along with our in-laws, we must unhook ourselves financially. We do not recommend that married children live with parents in order to save money. This financial arrangement can lead to too much reliance on parents. Nor do we recommend that parents loan money to their married children or offer to pay their way through school. If parents want to give their children gifts, that may be a different matter, but a loan can foster dependency, unwanted control from parents and, eventually, resentment on both ends. Parents need to make sure their gifts are given with no strings attached.

If a couple is married and relying on parents to cosign for their mortgage, to decorate their nursery, to finance their vacations or to give their children college educations, they need to reconsider the unfair burden of expectation they are placing on their in-laws. Parents must not feel guilty helping their children gain financial independence. It's part of the God-given principle of leaving.

Physical Dependence

The cord of physical dependence on parents must also be cut. This entails, of course, physically leaving and moving to a new home. If either husband or wife has not been fully emancipated from the parents, we suggest to couples that it may not be best to live near their parents, at least until this issue is resolved. Their relationship may get off to a better start if they move out of town for the early years of their marriage, giving them a chance to develop physical independence. Autonomy is difficult for some mothers and fathers to grant, perhaps because of years of patterning, and close proximity may slow a newly married couple's efforts to become a separate family.

One woman writes of her experience in establishing her family as a newlywed:

> When I married fifty years ago, my parents were dead. I married a man who was also an orphan, so we had no role models of what in-laws should or should not be like. In the early years, there were times when I could have used a shoulder to cry on or someone who would listen to my woes; but having none, I was left to face my real or imaginary problems and find solutions with my spouse. As I got older, and wiser, I decided this was probably a blessing, and it has influenced the way we have treated our ten children and seven in-laws.

Shortly after we got married, we moved to Portland, Oregon, over two thousand miles away from Jorie's parents in the Chicago area and some six hundred miles from Ron's parents in the San Francisco area. This decision was not a conscious choice to move away from our families; it was a ministry opportunity we felt God was leading us to.

The first few months of our marriage were difficult for Jorie because she was so far from her parents in Chicago, where she had spent the first twenty years of her life. We loved each other dearly, but she was really homesick. So we decided that Jorie should fly back to Chicago by herself once a year to give her time to spend alone with her parents. In addition, we also agreed to vacation each summer at her parents' home on Lake Michigan. This allowed Jorie time to catch up with her parents. The rest of the year we learned to rely on each other in a way which probably would not have happened had we lived close to either of our families.

Although it was difficult having none of our parents nearby, in retrospect we feel that being away from our parents helped us to bond more quickly as a couple, cleave to one another and establish our own family. If parents are aware that it is important for a young couple to establish independence physically, it is possible to do so even while living in the same home. But this is an extra challenge needing full cooperation by the children and both sets of parents-in-law.

In establishing physical independence, also beware of relying too heavily on parents to provide regular child care. Many couples we know expect their parents to provide regular—and free—baby-sitting. But parents with grown children have spent twenty or more years actively parenting, and it is neither their duty nor their obligation to help parent their grandchildren. Some grandparents have the time and desire to actively participate. Others don't, or can't, and should not be pressured into feeling guilty for this decision. If grandparents want to help with grandchildren, it is better for them to volunteer, setting parameters under which they feel comfortable. If grandparents do not volunteer, it is probably best that married children not ask for their help. The truth is that grandparents' baby-sitting may be convenient and cheap, but it can set the stage for problems (see chapter eight).

If you as children are depending on your parents for either financial or child-rearing assistance, it can damage the adult-to-adult relationship you need to have with your parents. You may revert to a parent-child relationship, which can put you at odds with your spouse.

Emotional Dependence

Moving across country, of course, does not ensure that the newly married couple will live out the biblical admonition to "leave father and mother." Although separated by thousands of miles, children can still be dependent on parents emotionally. Leaving implies a relinquishment of emotional dependence as well. A continued emotional reliance on parents decreases the likelihood of bonding in the marriage relationship. We know some men and women who call or visit their parents to discuss key issues in their lives which they have not yet discussed with their mate. They give their affection to, receive their security from and express most of their creative personality with their parents. Such a pattern is extremely painful for the mate and damaging to the marriage. If cleaving is to occur, our first emotional bond must be with our spouse, not with our parents.

A mother may miss her last child so much that she inadvertently causes her child's spouse to resent her as an interfering in-law, even though she has no intention of hurting her child's marriage. A son may value his father's financial expertise so much that he seeks his advice before making any of his own investments. This can cause his wife to feel left out of the decision-making and resentful toward her father-in-law. In this case, the son is the key factor. It's not wrong for him to seek his father's advice, but he needs to take special care that that relationship does not supersede his relationship with his wife. He and his wife must make the final decision together.

When couples are committed to making their marital bond top priority, they must agree to never share intimate needs or decisions with either set of parents without their mate's permission. A couple must build their lives together, and everything should be kept private unless agreed otherwise. They must turn to each other as the primary source of their emotional support. When both sets of parents and married children realize and respect these truths, all individuals have freedom to build healthy friendships without the fear of unhealthy emotional dependence.

Parental Approval

A married person's first priority must be to seek the approval of his or her mate. Some mates are so dependent on their parents' approval that this need discourages the new marriage relationship. Spouses who perform to please their mothers or fathers more than their mates may strive to clean house the way their mom would want or discipline the children with their dad in mind, hoping for their recognition or approval. Such actions will threaten their mates' sense of security.

One woman said that every time she and her husband bought a house, her mother's approval would be on her mind. She wasn't really free to make a decision with just her family's needs in view. Men who work for or with their fathers can do the same thing. A man's misdirected dependence on his parents can diminish his wife's sense of self-worth.

In the early years of our marriage, I felt a number of times that it was more important for Jorie to get her parents' approval than mine. Sometimes when Jorie and I visited them at their lake house we would make plans to play tennis, go to the beach or go out to dinner. When Jorie would share our plans with her parents, they would express disapproval because they had other plans for us for that particular day. Jorie would then ask me if we could change our plans. I would become frustrated, worrying that she cared more about pleasing her parents than pleasing me. That thought was threatening to me. It caused me to feel I had to compete with Jorie's parents for her love. Although Jorie loves me as her best friend and also loves her parents dearly, my perception of what was happening put tension in our marriage and on my relationship with my in-laws.

It was only as Jorie assured me that our marriage relationship took precedence over her relationship with her parents that the tension subsided. Assured of the priority I had in Jorie's life, I became able to relax and be more open to schedule changes initiated by her parents. If you are married, the approval of your spouse should be your most important consideration.

Before visiting parents, especially in the early years of marriage, it is wise for a couple to agree about the length of time they will stay. If parents want you to stay longer than that, tell them of your previous decision. Getting their approval, though important, should not be the number-one priority. Or, if one of you would like to stay longer, you may be comfortable deciding that the other will go home a few days earlier.

One man, Mick, told me that he and his wife disagree over how often to see her parents. He prefers to see them only a couple of times a month. Jen's parents want to visit two to three times every week. This disagreement has led to dishonesty in the couple's relationship. Since Jen knows that Mick does not approve of so much contact, she sees or calls her parents secretly. She doesn't like the deception, but she doesn't know what else to do.

Once we establish the biblical principle that our relationship with our mate takes priority over all our other relationships, we are on our way to finding a solution to such conflicts. God's way shows us that gaining our parents' approval cannot be our top concern; spousal approval must be primary. So in the previous example, Jen and Mick would do well to come to an agreement as to how many times each month they will see Jen's parents. Then they can discuss the possibility of her seeing or talking to them additional times on her own. If she has helped Mick understand that her relationship with him is second only to her relationship with Christ, chances are Mick won't feel threatened by her desire to spend time with her family.

In addition, if Jen's parents help Mick understand that they want their daughter's marriage to take precedence over their relationship with her, he will not need to fret over their time spent together. As they all understand God's principles and communicate those principles in tangible ways to each other, they can spend time together without anyone feeling threatened.

Parents Helping Their Children Leave
To foster oneness in their children's marriages and to show that they respect the biblical principle of leaving and cleaving, parents must recognize that their role is to stand beside them, not between.

Jean Parvin tells the story of her mother-in-law, who had determined to allow her son to leave.

We had only been married for two weeks when we visited Bill's parents. Imagine my surprise when Bill's mother asked me how he wanted his eggs fixed! She had fixed his breakfast for more than twenty years, yet she deferred to me.[1]

Bill's mother was off to a great start as a mother-in-law. She wanted to make it clear that she recognized her son's leaving and that his primary and closest relationship must be with his wife.

It may not be easy for parents to stand beside their children and encourage them to make pleasing their spouse their first priority. But, easy or not, it's critical to the task of being a great and godly mother- or father-in-law.

We spent the first few months of our marriage in Chicago while Ron finished seminary. One day, after we had had a minor disagreement in the morning, Jorie drove to her mom's house after a full day of teaching instead of driving straight home. Jorie went hoping to receive sympathy, but instead her mom said, "You can't stay here. You go home now and work things out." Wisely, she didn't come between husband and wife. Although mother and daughter are very close, I'm grateful for an in-law who knows that our marriage must take precedence even over the close friendship of a mother and daughter. To stand by your children in a loving and noncontrolling way takes a great deal of discipline. It's difficult to stand by and watch them make mistakes or get hurt.

We must recognize that the admonition to leave is not directed just to children. Parents-in-law must help in allowing their children to leave physically and emotionally. In Mark 10 Jesus adds to his Father's words from Genesis by saying, "So they are no longer two, but one. Therefore what God has joined together, let man not separate" (vv. 8-9). Some parents act as if it is their mission to come between their child and their son- or daughter-in-law! They must be unaware that they are violating this teaching.

Whenever I conduct a wedding, I remind everyone that none of them are to come between the bride and groom.

One woman wrote to me regarding this subject.

Our marriage counselor did us a great favor by requiring both sets of our parents to sit down with him at our rehearsal. He firmly reminded the parents that their role was changing from parent to advisor—and that only when asked.

One way parents can observe the biblical principle of leaving is by giving their married children adult status. When they accept the truth that the job of parenting is over, they can begin relating to their children and their children's spouses on an adult level.

One mother made this transition from parent to friend smoothly because she allowed her children to leave.

They have made good choices in choosing their mates; they are good parents. They do not ask for advice, and I do not offer any. We have mutual respect for each other and are good friends.

Parents who want to keep the communication lines clear and avoid conflict with their married children and sons- and daughters-in-law would do well to observe the practical advice given by Dear Abby some time ago, entitled "How to Get Along with Your Daughter-in-Law."

1. When you telephone your son at his home and his wife answers the phone, do not say, "Is John there?" Spend a few minutes asking how she is—and what's new. And if they live out of town, when you write a letter, always address it to both your son and his wife.

2. If your son was previously married, don't bring up his past marriage. And if he's had girlfriends in the past, don't mention them, either. If your daughter-in-law has been previously married and has children by that marriage, accept these grandchildren as your own. Don't play favorites.

3. Never offer advice unless it's asked for. Never criticize your daughter-in-law's cooking, housekeeping, children, friends or new hairdo. And don't try to rearrange her furniture.

4. Display pictures that include her and her children. Every time she looks at them, it will make her feel wonderful.

5. Never say, "John looks thin" or "pale" or "tired." His wife will take it as a personal insult.

6. If your daughter-in-law has given you a gift, be sure to display it or wear it (at least once) regardless of how much you dislike it.

7. Never repeat family gossip. And try not to listen to any.

8. Never allow your son—or his wife—in the heat of anger to tell you something unkind about the other. They will eventually kiss and

make up, and you will be left holding the dirty laundry.

9. If they are childless, don't harp on how much you'd like to have grandchildren. Some couples are not ready; some couples may have been trying for a long time without success; and some couples do not want children—which is strictly their business.

10. One cardinal rule: Regardless of how close you live to each other, never drop in without calling first. (A telephone call from the corner drugstore is all it takes.)

11. If perchance she has said something to hurt your feelings, don't let it fester; take it up with her—don't complain to your son.

12. Do not monopolize the holidays. Remember, your daughter-in-law has parents, siblings and friends she may want to spend time with on the holidays. Some couples may prefer spending an occasional holiday by themselves.

13. Let your son go. Recognize him for the adult he is; stop calling him Sonny, Junior or any other juvenile nickname he has long outgrown.

14. If you have other daughters-in-law, treat them equally. And that goes for their children too.[2]

Cleaving to Your Spouse

Leaving parents comprises only the first half of God's advice. "For this reason a man will leave his father and mother and be united to his wife, and they will become one flesh" (Gen 2:24). The King James Version says that the husband "shall cleave unto his wife." It's not enough to leave our parents; we must cleave to our mate.

Interestingly, cleaving to and genuinely loving your mate is one of the finest ways to bond with your in-laws. The heartfelt desire of most parents is to see their married son or daughter loved and cared for. If they sense that you are providing this kind of nurture, in most cases they will welcome you with open arms and will embrace you as one of the family. But if they sense that you are not fulfilling your vow of love to their son or daughter, animosity can arise instantly. One mother writes to her son-in-law,

> As you marry my daughter and start your life together, one piece of advice I want to give to you is to *love* her—no matter what. She isn't perfect. She has her moods, attitudes and opinions. You will not agree with her some of the time. You may not even *like* her sometimes. But *never* stop loving her.

The literal sense of the Hebrew word for "be united" or "to cleave" is to "stick to" or "be glued to" a person. Husband and wife are glued together like two pieces of paper. If you try to separate two pieces of paper that are glued together, you will tear them both. If you try to separate a husband and wife who are cleaving together, both will be hurt.

Husbands and wives are to cleave together and become one flesh. God's equation is not $1 + 1 = 2$ but $1 + 1 = 1$. A husband and wife are to become one spiritually, emotionally and physically, which is a lifetime process. This oneness involves sharing the same home and the same worldly goods, being parents of the same children and being partners in joy and sorrow. Wise in-laws realize that they give a gift to themselves by doing all they can to strengthen and support this process in their children's lives.

What practices can we cultivate that will help us cleave to our spouse, unite with and bond to our mate?

Friendship

The first element essential in cleaving to our mates is *friendship*. Solomon writes, "[Wisdom] will save you also from the adulteress, from the wayward wife with her seductive words, who has left the partner of her youth and ignored the covenant she made before God" (Prov 2:16). The Hebrew word *'allûp*, translated "partner," is a term used to describe the closest of friends. We are entreated by Scripture to enjoy our mates as best friends: "May you rejoice in the wife of your youth" (Prov 5:18).

Jorie and I usually spend at least one hour together each night after all the kids go to bed, relating the day's activities and sharing our feelings. We also try to go to bed at the same time. For twenty years we have gone on a date once a week, usually playing tennis together, going to dinner or watching a movie. We have to spend at least this much time together if we hope to continue to be best friends.

Sometimes we have left on our date with children hanging on to our legs crying for us to stay home, but we have realized that nurturing our relationship is vital to our whole family's welfare. I also try to take Jorie, without kids or responsibilities, on one weekend and one week-long getaway each year to further nurture our relationship. We try to follow the pattern of one hour per day, one day per week and one weekend per year alone together to help us cleave together as friends.

When Jorie met me, my two favorite sports were water skiing and tennis. If I have leisure time I would rather water ski or play tennis than sit and talk. Jorie didn't give a rip about water skiing, but she learned to ski well so she could be with me. She also took tennis lessons and joined some tennis teams. We now love playing together. Because she took the time to become proficient at the sports I love, we spend far more time together than we would have if she hadn't made that investment of her time and energy.

If your spouse golfs, it's worth trying your hand at golf. If her hobby is downhill skiing, hit the slopes. (If it's bungee jumping or shooting rats at the dump, then you have a problem!) The point is, it's worth investigating areas where you can spend time together so you become best friends. Can a marriage succeed without common interests? Yes, but with all the challenges every marriage faces anyway, the more commonalities you share, the faster you will learn to cleave.

Another practice important to a couple trying to forge a friendship is an agreement to make decisions together. This does not mean that a couple should never consult parents for advice regarding decisions. Partners who cleave together do not have to reject their parents. Instead, couples who cleave together as best friends are more secure in their relationship, so they are less threatened by input from parents and parents-in-law.

Faithfulness

Another element essential to cleaving is *faithfulness*. Every year hundreds of married partners are shocked to learn that their mate has become embroiled in an affair. "It could never happen to me," they said, but suddenly they find they're experiencing terrible pain. Unfortunately, Christians and those with outwardly stable marriages are not exempt.

The adulterous relationship hurts, but it is the accompanying deceit, dishonesty and disloyalty that shatter the marriage and threaten the self-esteem of the violated partner. "How could you deceive me like this?" a husband or wife might ask. "How could you lie to me? How could you mock my trust?"

Lack of security in a mate's faithfulness can destroy love and cleaving faster than any other element. In contrast, commitment between partners, so that each partner knows he or she is number one, is one of the finest magnets to draw lovers together. Scripture extols marriage, which Solomon emphasizes in Proverbs 5:15-20:

Drink water from your own cistern, running water from your own well. Should your springs overflow in the streets, your streams of water in the public squares? Let them be yours alone, never to be shared with strangers. May your fountain be blessed, and may you rejoice in the wife of your youth. A loving doe, a graceful deer—may her breasts satisfy you always, may you ever be captivated by her love. Why be captivated, my son, by an adulteress? Why embrace the bosom of another man's wife?

It is far more fulfilling, he argues, to be forever infatuated with the wife of your youth.

Again he writes, "But a man who commits adultery lacks judgment; whoever does so destroys himself. Blows and disgrace are his lot, and his shame will never be wiped away" (Prov 6:32-33). The adulterous man and unfaithful woman destroy themselves.

It's crucial that in-laws understand this most basic principle of marriage so that they can all do what they can to protect the marriage they are related to. How can we foster faithfulness and guard against unfaithfulness?

First, we all need to *protect our mates.* We protect them from unfaithfulness by doing the best job we can to meet their needs. When deep human needs are left unmet for a period of time, the door to infidelity swings wide open. When things aren't going well in your marriage, other people may begin to look more attractive than your own spouse. If you want to protect your mate from adultery, see to it that you are so sensitive, so caring, so loving, such a good parent and so attentive sexually that your mate wouldn't think of looking elsewhere.

Parents and parents-in-law can be a tremendous help in this delicate area. Parents can encourage their sons to remember their wives' birthdays and other special days, for example. We have a plan for the future. When our children marry—if our health allows—we want to give one week of free baby-sitting to each of their families each year, so our children can get away for a week with their mate. This gift may be in lieu of bought gifts for Christmas or birthdays.

Second, *keep your marriage alive.* Adultery, in practically all cases, happens to people who have allowed their marriage to go stale. Dorothy Sayers, in her fascinating book *Christian Letters in a Post-Christian Age*, divides the seven deadly sins into "hot" sins and "cold" sins. She classifies adultery as a "cold" sin. Fornication, sexual activity between unmarried people, is a "hot" sin, but adultery is a "cold" sin. It happens to stale people, to people who are weary and worn out. It happens to people with unsatisfactory marriages and unlimited opportunity. When they find someone who cares, appreciates them and looks great, they're on the slippery slope to disaster.

If you suffer from a poor physical relationship in your marriage, more than likely it indicates broken communication patterns or a lack of devotion, respect and trust. But you can't leave it that way. Scripture teaches that husbands and wives have a duty to fulfill each other sexually. It is vital to meet our partner's sexual needs so completely that he or she will have no desire to look elsewhere. A healthy physical relationship usually indicates open communication lines and a high degree of loyalty and mutual support. How do you get your marriage to that point? You have to put energy into it. It takes work to be faithful.

Are you committed to complete faithfulness to your mate? Such commitment is not impossible in our day of sexual permissiveness. *The Social Organization of Sexuality* reveals that 94 percent of married Americans are faithful to their spouses. Eighty-three percent of all adults have one or zero sex partners a year. Adultery is the exception in America. Nearly 75 percent of married men and 85 percent of married women say they have never been unfaithful.[3] You can be faithful too. It's worth working on. And parents and parents-in-law can give their children a tremendous gift by praying for their children to be faithful to each other.

Love for the Lord

The third essential element that helps partners cleave to one another is *love for the Lord.* The first step in becoming a wise husband or wife is to love the Lord. If we are right with God, he enables us to get right with our mate. The greatest gift you can give your spouse is to love God. Your in-laws will find it easier to trust you, as well, if you love and obey God.

A practice that can help all of us who are married to love God is praying together. Nothing bares our souls to someone else as quickly as heartfelt prayer. I do not know any couple who regularly prays together who is not growing deeper in understanding and oneness. Prayer has bonded Jorie and me together as a couple. Jorie tells me she gets to know me better when we pray. Hearing me pray gives her a window into my deepest feelings.

Grace

A fourth essential element in learning to cleave in a healthy and harmonious marriage is *grace.* Grace is the oil that lessens friction in marriage. It is the willingness to overlook faults, the readiness to forgive, the inclination to serve, the disposition to submit for the good of the marriage. Grace is the opposite of a critical spirit.

Solomon suggests there is nothing worse than living with a contentious person. He writes, "Better a dry crust with peace and quiet than a house full of feasting, with strife"; "better to live on a corner of the roof than share a house with a quarrelsome wife"; and "a quarrelsome wife is like a constant dripping on a rainy day" (Prov 17:1; 21:9; 27:15). Both husbands and wives can develop angry or quarrelsome dispositions and fall into the habit of nagging. But even if it is our lot to have landed a critical mate, God's way for us is to respond with grace.

How can we respond to our mates with grace? Or, if we tend to be negative ourselves, how can we overcome a nagging and critical spirit? It takes grace. Grace to accept. Grace to overlook. Grace to forgive, to be kind, to yield one's own rights, to affirm. Grace to live unselfishly. One person said, "The key to a healthy marriage is to keep your eyes wide open before you wed and half closed thereafter." At first glance it appears that the person who lives by grace loses and is taken advantage of. But the person who lives by grace wins, for grace is the oil that keeps life running smoothly.

Grace can help us affirm our mates rather than criticize them. If we are to cleave together, we must break the tendency to criticize. Constant criticism tears away at the process of becoming one. Husbands and wives are gravely mistaken if they think it is their job to remake their mate. Ruth Graham, wife of evangelist Billy Graham, once wisely said: "It's my job to love Billy. It's God's job to make him good." If we replace the name Billy with the name of our mate, we are closer to understanding the concept of grace.

The psalmist tells us,

> He [God] does not treat us as our sins deserve or repay us according to our iniquities. For as high as the heavens are above the earth, so great is his love for those who fear him; as far as the east is from the west, so far has he removed our transgressions from us. (Ps 103:10-12)

God does not treat us according to our sins, but chooses to be compassionate and overlook many, perhaps most, of the things we do wrong. He treats us with grace. Most of our marriages would be transformed if we gave our mates the same forgiveness.

Where do we get this grace to affirm rather than criticize? We receive it from Jesus Christ. Paul writes, "Get rid of all bitterness, rage and anger, brawling and slander, along with every form of malice. Be kind and compassionate to one another, forgiving each other, just as in Christ God forgave you" (Eph 4:31-32). We are to practice grace toward our mate just as Christ has been gracious with us. We are admonished to treat others the way Christ has treated us.

If your parents or in-laws ever make a critical statement about your mate, I suggest that you respond with a strong but loving rebuff, keeping in mind that it is our scriptural obligation to protect our marriage and cleave to our mates.

Don Meredith, in his book *Becoming One*, tells of a man whose mother was just leading up to a critical remark about his wife. He interrupted with, "Mom, I love you a lot, but please don't be critical of Joan. I want you to know she is God's gift to me, and I don't want to hear those criticisms." His mother hastily replied, "Don't be silly; I wasn't going to be critical of her." The wise son responded with, "Forgive me, Mom. I just so want you and Joan to be friends, because I love you both so much." He was strong but kind to his mother.[4]

To Sum Up

Marriage involves far more than two people. It is the bringing together of two families. We must realize the importance of leaving our parents and cleaving to our spouse in obedience to the Lord's command for a healthy and faithful marriage. Devotion to the Lord is critical to building a happy marriage and building rapport with our in-laws. Resolve never to become a wedge in your in-laws' marriage. Instead, help them cleave to one another. By God's grace we can experience a loving, Christ-centered marriage and a satisfying relationship with our in-laws.

Questions for Reflection or Discussion

1. Read Genesis 2:24. Why do you think God commanded sons and daughters to leave their parents and be united with their spouses?

2. Why is leaving critical to a healthy marriage?

3. What are some ways parents of married children can violate God's principle of leaving and make it more difficult for their married children to leave?

4. How does a couple's cleaving together and developing a strong marriage

help their relationships with their in-laws?

5. Why is it important for a husband and wife to become best friends? What are some practices husbands and wives can follow to become better friends?

6. Why is grace important to a marriage? How is grace important to in-law relationships?

7. What principle or insight in this chapter was most helpful to you?

5
Beating the Urge to Control

O *ne husband confessed to me:*

My in-laws feel they have lost Karen to me. I feel like they are always trying to control us. They want to prove to me that they love Karen more than I do, they know her better than I do, and that she loves them more than me. What bothers me as much as anything is that in their efforts to control, they show no respect for boundaries in our marriage.

These parents would make plans that would force their daughter to be with them or to choose between something her husband wanted her to do and something they wanted her to do. When she would choose to comply with her parents' plan for her, they would use that as proof that she really loved them more than her husband. Whenever her husband would make plans that would take her away from them or which they disapproved of, they would try to discourage her from proceeding. If she agreed with them, they would use it as further evidence that they knew her better than he did or that she loved them more than him.

The urge to control others is one of the most blatant but common violations of the biblical principle of leaving and cleaving. How can we suppress this urge? This is where our faith is invaluable.

Principle Four: Trusting God's Sovereignty Reduces the Need to Control In-Laws

When we believe that God is sovereign and that he works all things together for good, trusting in his sovereignty reduces our need to control people. We can trust God's sovereign hand in our child's choice of a mate or a parent's remarriage. We can place our trust in God's providence to heal a struggling marriage of a son or daughter, or to bring good out of a difficult in-law relationship. Trust sets us free to love people, which is exactly what God has called us to do.

What do we mean by the sovereignty of God? When we ascribe sovereignty to our great God and Creator, we acknowledge that he is the supreme power and authority in the universe. Nothing takes place without his permission.

Paul tells us, "And we know that in all things God works for the good of those who love him, who have been called according to his purpose" (Rom 8:28). Believers have the privilege of knowing not only that we are loved by a powerful God who is with us, but also that this God causes all things to work for good. So we can relax and don't have to control everything or everyone in our lives.

Trusting God's sovereignty does not come naturally for all people. Many of us find it difficult to put our full trust in God. Instead we feel that we have to take matters into our own hands. Applying the principle we discuss in this chapter requires an emotional and spiritual maturity that is rare. Newly married children may not have the Christian maturity to fully trust God in their in-law relationships. In these cases we believe it is the responsibility of parents, when they have greater maturity in Christ, to set the example of living out this biblical principle. In cases where the children are stronger in faith, they must lead by example. Using the assumption that in most cases parents have known Christ longer and grown further in faith, we have pointed most of our examples in this chapter to parents.

Trust in God's sovereignty can help us avoid at least four dangerous controlling behaviors that can damage, if not destroy, our in-law relationships: *worry, second-guessing, judging* and *competition.*

Worry

One practice that can create friction in in-law relationships is *worry.* Worry puts stress on the worriers and on others involved. Parents and parents-in-law worry about their children and children-in-law more often than the reverse, but it can happen both ways.

One mother worried constantly about the health of her adult daughter, who had been married for many years. She sent her vitamins, made doctor appointments for her and continually called to inquire after her health—and the daughter enjoyed good health. Imagine the stress this mother put on her child's marriage, perhaps unintentionally, by worrying about her daughter (and, implied, about her son-in-law's ability to make wise decisions regarding health!). What a contrast to parents whose missionary children serve in a country without pure water, adequate food inspection or medical care, but who believe God will protect them because he has a purpose for their being there. When we really believe God is in control, we can relax.

Another couple was extremely worried about their grandchildren's involvement in Little League baseball, feeling it put the children under too much pressure at too young an age. The grandchildren loved playing, and their parents monitored carefully to make sure the game was a positive experience. But the grandparents continually voiced their disapproval and put pressure on them to take the children out of baseball. Tension was great.

A solution appeared, however, when the parents sat the grandparents down to discuss the situation. They told their parents that they realized there is a high degree of pressure in all sports today. After assuring the grandparents that they were trying to protect the grandchildren from undue pressure, they asked them if they would pray for them. From that point on, the grandparents prayed for their grandkids instead of worrying about them. They began to rest in God's sovereignty, realizing that God was in control and could work through their children to help them make wise decisions regarding the grandchildren.

In another situation, a daughter-in-law worried that her mother-in-law would ruin her privacy, her marriage and her relationship with her children if the widowed mother-in-law moved in with them. Although the family had assessed the options together and determined that this move was the best option, the daughter-in-law was certain that her life was ruined. Before the mother-in-law even moved in, the daughter-in-law was resentful of her stolen privacy and her husband's unfairness in pressuring her to take his mother in. Lacking God's foresight, she didn't realize what a help her mother-in-law would become in cooking, cleaning and nurturing the grandchildren. There was conflict in their relationship because of the daughter-in-law's resentment and lack of trust in God. Only when the younger woman began to recognize God's hand in her living situation did she begin to appreciate the good her mother-in-law brought to the family.

We should all worry less and pray more! God is in control, whether or not we choose to acknowledge it. We could all relax more if we really believed and put into practice this truth.

In the Sermon on the Mount, Jesus tells us that we don't need to worry, because our Father in heaven will take care of us.

Therefore I tell you, do not worry about your life, what you will eat or drink; or about your body, what you will wear. Is not life more important than food, and the body more important than clothes? Look at the birds of the air; they do not sow or reap or store away in barns, and yet your heavenly Father feeds them. Are you not much more valuable than they? Who of you by worrying can add a single hour to his life?

And why do you worry about clothes? See how the lilies of the field grow. They do not labor or spin. Yet I tell you that not even Solomon in all his splendor was dressed like one of these. If that is how God clothes the grass of the field, which is here today and tomorrow is thrown into the fire, will he not much more clothe you, O you of little faith? So do not worry, saying, "What shall we eat?" or "What shall we drink?" or "What shall we wear?" For the pagans run after all these things, and your heavenly Father knows that you need them. But seek first his kingdom and his righteousness, and all these things will be given to you as well. (Mt 6:25-33)

Suppose you go to a party and see a buffet of all kinds of wonderful foods. Looking over the delectable treats makes your mouth water. But you also notice a seemingly endless stream of people waiting in the buffet line ahead of you, and you start to worry that you won't get any food. So what do you do? You cut in line and start grabbing shrimp and sandwiches and cashews and cramming them into your mouth, and you begin stuffing delicacies into your pockets. Rather than trusting in the provision of your host, you take matters into your own hands.

Now suppose, instead, as you enter the party, the host comes to you and says, "Hello, my dear friend. I'm so glad you came. I know how you love cashews, so I have a jar saved for you in the kitchen. And I kept back a whole sour cream raisin pie for you, since I know it's your favorite. Before you leave, come by the kitchen and I'll give them to you." This would change your attitude to the whole party, wouldn't it? You would be free to be expansive and generous with others. You could encourage them to try the various foods because you knew the host was taking care of you.

We don't need to worry about whether we'll get enough, for our Father in heaven knows our needs and has promised to take care of us. We don't need to covet. We don't need to claw to get things for ourselves and clutch all we have with a tight fist. Jesus promises that if we put God and his kingdom first, we can rest content that he'll take care of us. We can hold on loosely to whatever God gives us because we know there's plenty more where it came from. There's an inexhaustible supply! We're free to share generously with others, for we know God will take care of us and give us all that we need. And we don't have to control others in order to look out for ourselves.

There's a powerful relationship between this principle and the relationships we have with our in-laws. We don't have to control our in-laws, manipulate them to meet our needs or change them into the kind of people we want them to be. Instead, we can accept them the way they are and love them for who they are. We don't have to worry about our in-laws corrupting our son, daughter, mother or father, or ruining our own marriage. If we have been looking to God for guidance in all our decisions, we can trust that he has sovereignly placed us in the right in-law family.

If we really understand that God is sovereign and believe that he gives guidance to us as individuals, we don't have to question every decision our in-laws make. Though our children are no longer under parental authority, God will still give them guidance and will ultimately work things out the way he wants to. If we, parents or parents-in-law, don't have a clear picture of God's sovereignty, we may be tempted to fight to control our children when they marry because we consider ourselves wiser than they. But if we believe that God is constantly guiding and directing our children's marriages himself because he is sovereign, we can relax. We can allow our children to make decisions without worrying over their every move.

Second-Guessing

A second behavior pattern that brings trouble is *second-guessing.* Parents-in-law so badly want to see their children's marriages succeed, and they are desperately fearful it won't happen without their influence. But when parents and parents-in-law question their kids' every decision, they can alienate the younger couple. Their children will interpret this as a lack of trust in their decision-making ability—which it is. But second-guessing our married children's decisions also symbolizes a lack of trust in God's sovereignty.

Solomon, under the inspiration of the Holy Spirit, instructs us, "Trust in the LORD with all your heart and lean not on your own understanding; in all your ways acknowledge him, and he will make your paths straight" (Prov 3:5-6). If I have taught my children to trust in the Lord and follow his leading, then I can claim this promise for them. God will make their paths straight. He will lead them in the way they should go.

James offers similar encouragement. "If any of you lacks wisdom, he should ask God, who gives generously to all without finding fault, and it will be given to him" (Jas 1:5). If we have taught our children to go to the Lord when they need wisdom, then we have the assurance that God will generously provide it. We can trust that our children will be led by God in their choices, and we don't need to second-guess their decisions.

Jorie had a good friend in college whose father was a professor. Because her friend's family lived in the community, occasionally the girls would take a break from dorm life and visit them. One evening when Jorie and her friend were there, the mother announced that one of their daughters was returning home from Europe and would be bringing her fiancé, whom the family had never met. When Jorie asked the mom how she felt about one of her girls making a decision to marry a man they had never met, her answer surprised Jorie. She said that she had begun praying for her daughters' future husbands when each of the girls was a baby, and so when her daughter announced, "This is the one," she knew that he was! She didn't need to meet him, interview him or make this prospective son-in-law pass a test.

Her statement illustrated incredible trust in God's guidance and sovereignty for her five beautiful daughters. She trusted that whether or not she ever set eyes on the young men who would marry her most precious treasures, God would guide. Naive? No. Godly? Yes! We know she did her part. She had prayed faithfully for her daughters' mates for many years, had done her best to model a godly marriage to her children and had trained her daughters to know God and to depend on him for help in their lives.

This woman beat the urge to second-guess and control her children's choices, because she understood that we have a sovereign God—a God who guides us and unfolds his will. She knew that despite her best efforts to know everything about her children's future mates, she would never know as much about them as God does. Our best help to our children, better than any screening or interrogating, is to pray for God's guidance and will to unfold through them.

What a contrast to the wedding we know of where the mother of the bride wore black (before this day and age when it has become fashionable to wear black at weddings). The girl's parents didn't believe her boyfriend had the proper pedigree to make him a suitable match for their daughter. He did not have a well-to-do family, and his desire to pursue a career in ministry made him unacceptable to his future in-laws. The mother of the bride chose to announce her disapproval by wearing the traditional symbol of grieving at her daughter's wedding.

This mother-in-law started her in-law relationship at a tremendous disadvantage—one which she could have avoided. She may have been a strong believer in Christ, but she apparently failed to understand the meaning of God's sovereignty. She didn't trust that God was in control and fully capable of working out his purpose. Had she been able to believe the truth of Scripture, she could have saved herself from much stress and could have started out on a better footing with her son-in-law instead of inflicting terrible pain on them all.

As parents and parents-in-law, we don't have to question where our children choose to move, how many babies they have or what they spend on a house. Yes, parents should remain interested in their children's decisions. But instead of actively trying to influence the outcome, they should pray for these decisions and trust that God is even better equipped to guide than they are because he brings his eternal perspective to everything he does.

This principle also works in reverse. It's easy for adult children to second-guess the decisions of their parents or in-laws to remarry, move to a warmer climate or into a retirement home, or buy a new or second house. Trusting that God is sovereign leads children to pray more and question less the decisions of parents and parents-in-law.

Judging
A third element of control sometimes practiced by in-laws is *judging different parties involved in the relationship*. This usually includes a desire by one person to change someone else. In fact, this is probably

the biggest struggle in-laws have toward one another—the belief that things would be better "if only my father-in-law were different" or "if my daughter-in-law would just grow up." Many, perhaps most of us, are guilty of standing in judgment of our in-laws. We don't like them exactly the way they are, and we'd like them to change so we could like them better.

It's easy for this problem to surface, because whenever there are differences, there are often judgmental attitudes. One way is preferred over the other; my way is right and yours is wrong. Differences give us a basis for comparisons, and comparisons set the stage for judgments. And judgmental attitudes cause problems between people, especially when those people are in-laws.

Natural differences between parents-in-law and children-in-law can be monumental. To begin with, there is a generational difference of twenty or more years. That's big. Then there are differences in family backgrounds, such as financial status, ethnic traditions and denominational preferences. That's bigger! And the tendency, when there are differences between people, is to like *us* better than *them!*

We heard of a daughter-in-law who became so traumatized by the judgmental attitude of her in-laws that every time the in-laws came to visit, she suggested they eat out. She and her husband told his parents that they were in the habit of eating meals out, even though that wasn't true. The daughter-in-law simply did not want to cook for her in-laws, because her husband's mother was so particular about exactly how everything should be done that it could never be done well enough.

Should this daughter-in-law be pressured to cook in her mother-in-law's style? No. Are the mother-in-law's more formal and meticulous ways better than the daughter-in-law's? No. Differences are acceptable! When we believe the truth of Scripture that God is sovereign, that God is in control and that God made us as we are, we can resist the desire to change others—that tempting desire to make everyone just like us.

Where do differences come from? God. He made the diversity that we enjoy and sometimes resent. Differences are good, when we realize God made them. He, the Creator, could have made all people out of one pattern, millions and millions of clones of each other, but he didn't. It was he who created blue-eyed Scandinavians, wavy-haired Polynesians, doe-eyed Africans and dark-haired Chinese. All different, but all good.

It's not our job to judge or try to change those differences. Some prospective in-laws have chafed under the prospect of a son or daughter marrying outside their denomination, though both partners were solid believers. Others have lost sleep over a child marrying someone with less education. Still others have recoiled when children have selected mates of a different nationality or race.

Jesus tells us what our attitude toward one another should be: "Do not judge, or you too will be judged. For in the same way you judge others, you will be judged, and with the measure you use, it will be measured to you" (Mt 7:1-2).

As we seek to understand that God is sovereign and created all individuals, we can begin to give people the freedom to be who God created them to be, instead of trying to force them into the mold of our own expectations. The more differences there are between families of children who marry, the more adjustments will be needed in the process of becoming one. Differences present challenges, but *differences do not give any of us the freedom to judge other people.* In-laws who desire to be godly need to be conscious of this important fact.

So what do we do if our son marries a girl who is a strict vegetarian, and we're not? Do we make sarcastic comments at Thanksgiving or use subtle opportunities to scold her, showing our disapproval and fear for our son's and grandchildren's health? Not if we truly believe in God's sovereignty. If we know he created our daughter-in-law, we can resist the urge to try to change her. We can allow her the freedom to be who she is. We may be pleasantly surprised to see what she can fix for Thanksgiving dinner and to realize how happy and healthy she keeps our son.

In light of God's Word, doesn't it seem silly to go ballistic at not finding salt in your daughter-in-law's pantry or to criticize your father-in-law for watching too much television? So what if the daughter-in-law loves country pine furniture and the mother-in-law loves stately Mediterranean? How about if your son-in-law can't fix things around the house or your father-in-law can't golf? Or if one of you loves blue and the other brown? We know real cases where all of the above caused stress and conflict between parents-in-law and children-in-law.

God, in his sovereignty, created us with differences. If we trust him, we will seek to be content with the differences between us and our in-laws. If we wish to improve our relationship with our in-laws, we will resist the desire to judge and change them. We will grant them our blessing to be who they are and love them that way. So what if our daughter-in-law doesn't cook and clean? Our son chose her for her many other fine qualities. If that's good enough for him, that's good enough for us. Even though we know our son-in-law is spending money he and our daughter cannot afford, we still must refrain from judging him. We must pray for them; we may offer counsel if it is sought, but otherwise we must trust God to take care of things. Even when we learn that our son or daughter or son-in-law or daughter-in-law has been unfaithful, we must refrain from casting judgment. There are many factors to consider when evaluating adultery. We will continue to pray for them and believe that God can bring good out of a bad situation. Even when our child or child-in-law is not walking with the Lord, rather than passing judgment we should pray for them and show them our support.

We know one woman with four sons. As each of her sons married, she had plenty of opportunity to pass judgment on her daughters-in-law. Each of the women her boys chose was different from the others and quite different from the family. She could have passed judgment and criticized, attempting to make her daughters-in-law more like her. Instead she chose to accept them for who they were and love them unconditionally. This commitment required her to bite her tongue at times, but her willingness to love and accept them has paid off. As a result, she now has four daughters who love her dearly. We suspect that she has grown closer to some of her daughters-in-law than to her sons.

Sons- and daughters-in-law must also work hard at not being judgmental toward their parents-in-law. It's easy to be critical of the way they spend money, opinions they hold, activities in which they are involved, the way they raised their children or their lack of spirituality. We must remind ourselves that our sovereign God is able to take care of our in-laws. It is not our job to judge them but to accept and pray for them. All of us are guilty of being judgmental in some area of our in-laws' lives. We must seek to become people who are delightfully free of cattiness and criticism as we learn to appreciate the people God has brought into our lives.

Competition

Competition is a fourth element sometimes present in in-law conflict. Although it may not seem like a big problem, we have observed that it can absolutely destroy relationships between children and their in-laws.

The struggle most often verbalized is that between mother-in-law and daughter-in-law. Noted pediatrician T. Berry Brazelton aptly describes this problem.

> My grandmother had such an ample lap. I still remember the delicious feeling of sitting in it, surrounded by her extra-soft arms. As she rocked with me, the world seemed utterly safe.

When we were children, my siblings and I begged to stay overnight at Grandmother's house. It seemed as if she could nurture all of us—my grandfather, my father, my aunts and uncles, and all of us eleven grandchildren. I can still recall the day she said, "Berry's so good with babies!" That one comment from her showed me the mountain peak to which I have aspired ever since. I wanted to be a baby doctor then and now, just to please her. To this day, whenever I'm praised for my work, it's her voice I hear.

If only the nurturing she offered me could have been extended to my mother, we'd all have benefited. But as her daughter-in-law, my mother felt none of the support that I remember. Instead, my grandmother competed with her intensely for me, her first grandchild, and for my father, her first son.[1]

Sometimes competition shows up between parents-in-law. For example, if one set of in-laws is financially more well-to-do, the other set may feel threatened. These parents may in turn become possessive of their children, trying to even the score. They may demand an accounting of time spent together to make sure everything is fair and equal. They may jockey for holidays or for time with grandchildren. They may be envious of gifts the other set of in-laws received from the kids. We know one set of parents who demand an accounting of gifts received from the other in-laws, hoping to be able to compensate in some way and not lose out on the relationship. Competition between parents-in-law can put incredible tension on each set of parents and their children, and also on their children's marriage.

A woman shared with us recently through tear-filled eyes that her daughter and son-in-law's marriage was probably not going to make it. The biggest single factor in the demise of the marriage, she told us, is the other mother-in-law. She is a wealthy woman who uses her money as a means to control her son and exclude her daughter-in-law. The wealthy mother-in-law feared losing her son, so she would try to come between him and his wife by doling out money to him but giving nothing to her daughter-in-law. A widening split was caused in the couple's marriage.

If we know we're worthy in God's eyes, we don't need to compete with another set of in-laws for our children's attention in order to feel worthy.

If you notice competition between your two sets of parents, refuse to be partner to the competition, and seek understanding of how God's sovereignty applies to the situation. Try to love both sets of parents, focusing on appreciating their uniqueness and differences.

If you are a parent who may be competing with the other set of parents for your children's or grandchildren's love and attention, take this advice: Recognize the unfair stress it puts on your children's marriage, and *stop it*. Realize that there's no need for competition in any relationship, because our worth comes from God. Let's seek to love our family members and allow them the freedom to be who they are, without judging them or choosing favorites.

Grandparents want to love and be loved by their grandchildren. This is natural and expected. But sometimes grandparents compete with each other for affection and time spent with grandchildren. This can start as early as the grandchild's birth, concerning who goes into the hospital delivery room or who will stay with the young parents to lend a helping hand when they go home. Sometimes grandchildren foster this competition, proclaiming they like one grandmother better than the other.

Trusting God's sovereignty can once again help us minimize these conflicts. If we believe that God created us and knew what he was doing, we understand that we don't have to be in competition with anyone. We can accept that other people are different from us, and we are all wonderfully made.

One grandmother understood this concept well. When she went to pick up her young granddaughter one day, her granddaughter said, "Grandma Jean, Grandma Betty bought me a new doll. She bought me my new shorts and shirt and hair bow. Can we go shopping, Grandma Jean, and can you buy me things just like Grandma Betty?"

Instead of feeling threatened, the wise woman replied, "Grandma Betty is your shopping grandma. She takes you for very special shopping trips. But I'm your cookie-baking grandma. When we're together, I like to take you to my house so we can bake cookies, because I'm good at baking cookies. We can make chocolate chip cookies and roll sugar cookies and cut out hearts and stars and animals. It's okay if flour gets in our hair and colored sprinkles fall on the floor at your cookie-baking grandma's house. You're lucky you have a shopping grandma and a cookie-baking grandma."

What could have been escalating competition between grandparents for bigger and more expensive gifts was wisely averted. Grandma Jean understands the principle that people are different and is comfortable with who she is. Children need knitting grandmas and tennis-playing grandmas, musical grandpas and fishing grandpas. There can be story-reading grandmas, golfing grandmas, artistic grandmas, gardening grandpas and mechanically inclined grandpas. Whoever we are, God has designed us to have special input into the lives of our grandchildren. Parents and grandparents alike need to realize this important truth.

At times, parents-in-law and children-in-law will compete with each other. Instead of complimenting a daughter-in-law for cutting a new CD, one mother-in-law's response was, "When I record my first album, it's going to be . . ." This parent-in-law erroneously thought that she was in competition with her daughter-in-law. But she didn't have to be. The daughter-in-law's success had nothing to do with the mother-in-law's worth.

God in his sovereignty raises us up at the proper time. When we realize this, we can support all the successes of our in-laws without feeling threatened, because we aren't in charge of them—God is. There is no competition in God's eyes. This truth should help a daughter-in-law who pales next to a mother-in-law who exhibits her own art work; it should help a father-in-law who knows he will never travel as widely as his son-in-law has.

We hear the objection of those who ask, "But what about the in-laws who aren't Christians? Trusting in God's sovereignty is fine for the believer, but how will this help the person who doesn't even believe in God, let alone his providence?"

First, God's sovereignty is in no way dependent on our belief. God is not sweating it out in heaven waiting to read the latest Gallup poll as to how many people believe in him. He is in control whether or not we believe he is.

Second, to the believer, this doctrine is of incalculable value. It helps us avoid all kinds of frantic and unproductive attempts to control our mates or our in-laws. Instead it drives us to our knees, to the one true source of power. When we implement God's truth in our lives, believing that in his sovereignty he will lift us up at the proper time, all need for competition diminishes. If this has been an area where your relationship with your in-laws has struggled, resolve to minimize or end that urge to compete by trusting in God's sovereignty. Then seek to support that in-law in whatever successes—or failures—he or she experiences.

Questions for Reflection or Discussion

1. "The urge to control others is one of the most blatant but common violations of the biblical principle of leaving and cleaving." Do you agree or disagree with this statement? Why?

2. How does trust in God's sovereignty help us beat the urge to control others?

3. Read Matthew 6:25-33. How does Jesus' teaching help us overcome our

tendency to worry?

4. Read Proverbs 3:5-6, Romans 12:1-2 and James 1:5. How do these passages help us not to second-guess the decisions made by our in-laws?

5. Read Matthew 7:1-5 and Peter 2:22-25. According to these texts, why are we not to judge others?

6. What causes children-in-law to compete with parents-in-law and vice versa? How does trust in God's sovereignty help us overcome the need to compete with our in-laws?

7. What principle or insight in this chapter was most helpful to you?

6
Communication

*J*orie *has always been a master at* communicating. For example, once when we were vacationing on Lake Michigan, I took the kids to the beach for the afternoon while Jorie stayed home. She had a writing deadline hanging over her. Several hours later, the six kids and I strolled into the house, laughing and joking after a great time at the beach. Jorie had a glum look on her face. She had been doing laundry and making dinner preparations as well as writing. We asked her how she was. She said, "I feel like the family mule!" Nothing more needed to be said. We got the picture. It was time to get our act together and help out.

Principle Five: Communication Strengthens In-Law Relationships

No one can enjoy a healthy relationship with in-laws without regular and clear communication. There will be times when you will have to discuss sensitive subjects with your in-laws. Unless special care is given when communicating about these difficult topics, people can be deeply wounded. Good communication is a skill we can all benefit from if we're willing to invest the necessary energy to improve it.

Paul underscores an important principle for improving our communication in difficult situations. "Speaking the truth in love, we will in all things grow up into him who is the Head, that is, Christ" (Eph 4:15). Paul tells us to speak straight and honestly (the truth) within a context of sensitivity and kindness (love), and we can put this into practice when communicating with our in-laws.

Speaking in Love

Let's begin by outlining some different ways of "speaking . . . in love": communicating through bloodlines, communicating affirmingly and communicating as friends.

1. Communicate through bloodlines. One woman wrote to us about her struggles in communicating with her in-laws: "My husband provides little or no support, so I feel left to my own devices and stuck in a no-win in-law situation." Apparently her husband expected her to handle the difficult discussions with his parents.

Although it may be possible for a daughter-in-law to be the better communicator with her husband's parents, it is more likely that her relationship with her in-laws is more formal and less intimate than her husband's. If so, the husband should set the stage for good communication between them all. When communication with in-laws is strained in any way, the person with the closer and more intimate tie needs to be the bridge-builder and help improve communication between all parties. Observing this simple principle can significantly enhance communication between in-laws. We illustrate this idea as follows.

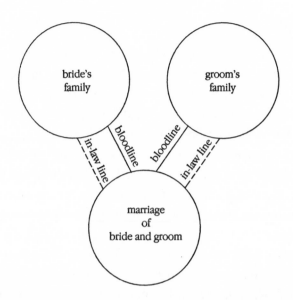

A husband and wife form a marriage that is the product of each of their families. The solid lines represent the blood relationship between the son and his parents and the daughter and her parents. The broken lines represent the relationship between the parents-in-law and the son- or daughter-in-law. It is natural, and expected, for the love and intimacy to be stronger between the child and parent than between the parent-in-law and child-in-law, especially at the beginning of a marriage relationship. In many cases parents meet their son's or daughter's prospective wife or husband only a few months or even weeks before the wedding.

Our goal in communicating with in-laws, as stated in chapter one, is that as our relationships strengthen, we seek to adopt our in-laws and graft them into our family. So the broken line of communication will grow into a solid, strong line. Until this happens, however, it is probably wise to handle sensitive or difficult communication between in-laws and married couples through the solid line—the blood or kinship line—rather than the in-law line.

Beth shared with us an example of how she and her husband, Lee, put this "blood-line" communication into practice. During the early years of her marriage, her in-laws would always answer every letter she wrote with a twenty-dollar bill enclosed in their response. The original idea had been to reward their kids for writing home during college. But now that Lee was married, this "encouragement" felt like bribery. Beth and Lee decided that the money should stop with marriage. It was at this point that their golden rule for dealing with families emerged: Any decisions they made as a couple that might prompt a negative response would be communicated to the respective family through the "blood" line. So when Lee's parents visited the next time, all the twenty-dollar bills they had sent were given back—by their son, with a careful explanation. Beth was not present. The money stopped, but the letters did not.

This couple discovered the wisdom of initiating difficult communication through the bloodline. This type of communication is necessary, especially where there is still a felt distinction between the role of "family" versus "in-laws." It is especially valuable in the early years of marriage, before the people involved have had a chance to graft as family, or if relationships are tense.

When our boys Tad and David were toddlers, there were a couple of times, while we were visiting my parents, when my father took the boys out without using their car seats. When his son was young, children did not have car seats, but today it's against the law for a child under five not to be in a car seat when riding in a car or truck. Yet when we asked my parents to use the car seats, they viewed our request as a bother, because they felt they had been careful parents without car seats. They responded, "The kids will be perfectly safe if we hold them in our arms." It upset us that they weren't willing to abide by our wishes.

How could we tactfully approach the problem? In this case Ron decided to talk to his dad. If Jorie had attempted to deal with him directly, it might have caused a rift in their relationship, but Ron could talk with him without serious danger of hurting his relationship with his parents. Ron didn't convince him that car seats were a necessity, and that was okay. But, realizing how important it was to us, his dad assured us that they would always use them in the future. After all, some things will simply remain generational differences.

One woman told us that each year she and her husband sit down and discuss their holiday plans as to which days should be spent with each set of parents. The issues include which family will get the "prime" days—and times. They always discuss, in the most loving way possible, how they want things to work out, trying to be aware of each family's habits and customs. Since they can only be in one place at a time, occasionally one family has to be turned down. In such a case, the kinship-line spouse lets the family know that they won't be able to be together for the holiday celebration.

Just as it is our goal to adopt our in-laws, our goal in communication should be that bloodlines disappear there as well. However, until we have truly grafted our in-laws as family, it may be helpful to remember that conflicts are resolved most easily when communication is initiated by people who share an intimate relationship.

2. Communicate affirmingly. Another way to speak lovingly with our in-laws is to use conversation as a means of building each other up, rather than as a tool to tear each other down.

At a recent church picnic we were lollygagging long after the last bits of food were gone. Wanting to include an elderly grandma figure in our aimless discussion, we asked her, "What advice would you give young people for getting along with their mothers-in-law?" Delighted to share wisdom gleaned from years of experience, she replied, "When I was a young bride, my mother-in-law said to me, 'I'll never say anything bad about you if you never say anything bad about me!' And she didn't, and I didn't, and we got along just fine!"

You could do nothing better than to resolve that you simply won't voice negative comments about your in-laws.

The writer to the Hebrews gives us terrific advice for communicating in a positive way: "Encourage one another daily, as long as it is called Today, so that none of you may be hardened by sin's deceitfulness" (3:13). If all married people gave their in-laws the promise that they would always encourage instead of discourage, very few would have in-law difficulties. We all hold power in our communication—power to criticize and tear down and power to affirm and build up. As we learn to better communicate with and about our in-laws, we will see our relationships begin to flourish.

You might say, "Such a suggestion works if your in-laws are nice— but mine aren't." What then? The truth of Scripture still stands. Just as we tell our children that it's their job to find some good in everyone they meet, it's our job to find the good in our in-laws and focus on that, regardless of how little we think that may be. If nothing else, sons- and daughters-in-law can focus on gratitude to the parents who birthed and raised the man or woman they fell in love with. And no matter what parents think of their son- or daughter-in-law, they can at least feel grateful that this son- or daughter-in-law has chosen to commit his or her life to their child. Our focus on positive communication can grow from this starting point.

A different way we can communicate affirmation is through touch. A gentle touch on the arm can communicate "I like you" or "I want to be close to you." Making it a practice to always greet your in-laws with a hug and kiss can be an important step in communicating love. Some families are comfortable with more touch than others, however, and a great deal of patience and flexibility needs to be exercised to accept family differences. If an in-law is not used to touch as a form of communication, the first response may very well be a stiffening or a pulling away. But if touching and hugging are perfectly natural and comfortable for you, try to include your in-laws in this display of physical affirmation. It could be one way to warm up a stiff or chilly relationship.

3. Communicate as friends. Relationships with our in-laws can improve when we communicate as friends rather than as parents and children. When we birth children, we are their parents from the time they are babies until we die. But the role we play in our children's lives and how we communicate within that role changes dramatically as our children mature. As we have said earlier, it is our role as parents to take our children from a place of total dependence on us to total independence as whole people. When our children reach adulthood, our training role ends.

This does not mean we have nothing more to teach our kids. We may be painfully aware of how little our grown children know about life. But when our children have left our home and established homes and families of their own, our parenting role diminishes greatly. That's all part of the biblical principle of leaving. Understanding this principle should change parents' styles of communication with their married children. We remain parents, but we must now learn to communicate with our married children as friends. To be successful in this new role we need to understand that our children are no longer accountable to us and we cannot make demands on them.

Most of us are very careful to treat our friends with respect. We may feel the freedom to give suggestions and advice, but we usually don't feel comfortable making demands on them. This principle also applies to our married children. We can support them and love them and hope that they will ask us for advice on gardening, income taxes, parenting or spot removal. But we need to approach giving advice, even needed advice, very carefully, just as we would with our adult friends.

We know a young couple who has virtually cut off all communication about important issues in their lives with one set of in-laws. They don't consult these parents about finances, jobs, house buying or child rearing, even though they want a good relationship with them. Every time they try to talk with these parents, the parents are very unsupportive and lecture them on how they're wrong. When the young couple told them of their excitement about a new house they were hoping to buy, the parents voiced their disapproval at how much time and energy would have to be expended in making the house livable. When this couple announced their delight about a new pregnancy, they learned that the in-laws didn't think they could handle a child. Finally, after several years of always feeling like "bad" children, they have learned to limit their talk with their in-laws to neutral subjects like the weather. This is a sad but common problem among in-laws.

This young couple could probably benefit greatly from the experience and wisdom of their parents, and the parents probably care deeply about their children and want to help them. But they have violated God's principle of leaving, forgetting that their role is now one of support and friendship. Parents and parents-in-law who deny this truth and dwell in the parent-to-child relationship will eventually strangle communication.

Married children have a responsibility in this area as well. Realizing that good parents will be hesitant to dump advice on them, adult children can help communication by asking questions of their parents when they want help. A wise son or daughter realizes there is much knowledge to be gained from the experience and expertise of his or her parents and parents-in-law. The door of open communication can be unlocked when married children are mature enough to ask questions of their in-laws, allowing them to share what they know.

Speaking the Truth

We have talked about the importance of communicating *with love* to our in-laws. Now we need to make a few comments about the other half of Paul's injunction about communication: *speaking the truth.* There are three excellent ways to communicate the truth to our in-laws, all biblically mandated for our own good and the good of others: communicate *honestly, directly* and *as a united front.*

1. Communicate honestly. If something our in-law has said or done has upset us and we feel strongly enough about it that we need to say something, it is very important to deal with the issue quickly. It's not fair to be really bothered by something but never mention it, and then let it surface years later in a moment of frustration. Our in-law will wonder why we didn't bring it up when it happened. Jesus tells us to "settle matters quickly with your adversary" (Mt 5:25). Harboring ill feelings leads to bitterness and creates distance in a relationship. Jesus' counsel is that if the issue is important enough to create distance in a relationship, then it's important enough to deal with quickly. Keeping short accounts is vital to healthy communication.

It's important, too, to limit your comments to the matter at hand, rather than recounting other irritations. Be careful not to begin generalizing and end up being more critical than you intended.

One of the toughest things to deal with in marriage is the special events with in-laws each year. The games played and power struggles encountered with brothers- or sisters-in-law are so unbearable that many actually dread the holidays, and it can be very difficult to communicate honestly with their in-laws about how they feel and why they are uncomfortable.

Janet always gave in to her husband's domineering mother regarding where the family would spend holidays. Then one year her mother-in-law insisted that everyone come to her home for Thanksgiving dinner—everyone except two people: her husband's eldest son, Tom, and Tom's fiancée. "I can't stand that girl," she explained.

Janet discussed the problem with her husband and won his reluctant agreement to confront her mother-in-law. "We are not spending Thanksgiving without Tom," she said firmly. "He and his fiancée will be here with us. You are welcome to join us if you wish."

Janet heard nothing until two days before Thanksgiving, when her mother-in-law announced that she was coming to Janet's gathering. "My resentment eased after that," Janet said. "I had taken a stand at last, and it paid off for everyone. We all ended up enjoying a happy Thanksgiving together."[1] Standing up for her beliefs and sharing them honestly and quickly led to a good result in this case.

2. Communicate directly. Speaking directly and clearly, instead of hinting around in order to make a thing less painful, is another way to speak the truth in love.

In Matthew 18:15 we are admonished, "If your brother sins against you, go and show him his fault, just between the two of you." Jesus counsels us to go to the offending person directly and alone. But remember: to communicate successfully, your purpose in going must be motivated by love, you must speak honestly, and you must do so with maturity and tact.

In chapter four we mentioned a "Dear Abby" column that shared tips for getting along with a daughter-in-law. In the interest of fair play, Abby offered the following day some similar tips on how to get along with your mother-in-law. One of her points especially illustrates the principle of direct communication: "If perchance [your mother-in-law] has hurt your feelings, don't let it fester and do not complain to your husband. Say, 'Mom, you hurt me,' then tell her why, so you can put the matter to rest."[2]

Although we have said that it is often best for sons and daughters to initiate communication with their own parents, Abby advises that if you have hurt feelings, you yourself ought to go to your mother- or father-in-law and deal with it quickly and directly. A mate can speak on behalf of a couple if the matter discussed pertains to the couple, but it is neither sensitive nor loving for a spouse to speak for his or her mate in an advocate role. Rather than complaining to your mate, who may not get an opportunity to deal with the issue quickly and may not have all the facts straight, it is often better to share your feelings directly with your in-law.

3. Communicate a united front. Critical to healthy, truthful communication with in-laws is the need for good communication between husband and wife. Jesus says, "For this reason a man will leave his father and mother and be united to his wife, and the two will become one flesh. So they are no longer two, but one" (Mk 10:7-8). This implies that couples are to communicate with each other and come to a meeting of their minds and thoughts. When spouses are in agreement, seldom will difficulties with in-laws come between them.

Some time ago Ron met in premarital counseling with Don and Sue, who confessed some concern about the relationship with their prospective in-laws. Sue had been invited by her fiancé's family to a family get-together celebrating Sue's ten-year-old son's birthday. The party was going well until Don's sister started a discussion about an estranged alcoholic brother. The various family members held divergent and strong opinions about how to deal with this wayward brother.

The discussion became very heated. Suddenly Sue ran into the bedroom and collapsed in a pool of tears. She couldn't believe that her prospective sister-in-law would be so rude as to ruin her son's birthday party by causing a fight. She asked Don if they could leave the party and go home. Don felt their sudden departure would only make things worse, and he asked her to pull herself together and stay for the evening. That he was more concerned about keeping peace with his family than pleasing her made Sue all the more distressed. She agreed to stay at the party, but the disagreement left some lingering doubts in her mind about whether he really loved her more than his family.

The best policy is to stand by our mate in all situations. By presenting a united front as a married couple, we demonstrate that we really love each other and agree on decisions. In doing this we are letting our in-laws know that their son or daughter makes us happy. We are demonstrating stability in a visible way to our in-laws.

A New Perspective

You may be encountering troubles in communicating with your in-laws. Perhaps you feel that you have the worst possible in-law situation. Maybe you need a change of perspective. Looking at your in-law relationship from a different perspective can revolutionize your communication with them. View the relationship from God's perspective—a chance to demonstrate the transforming power of Jesus Christ in your life.

What is God's perspective in your in-law relationship? What does he want you to learn from it? How does he want you to grow in this situation? Ask God to show you his perspective. Pray for his wisdom and insight and for the ability to see your in-laws as he sees them. He can even help you to be grateful for them someday. Imagine being *grateful* for your mother-in-law or daughter-in-law! A change of perspective can change the way you view your in-laws, so why not make it a permanent change of attitude?

Questions for Reflection or Discussion

1. The authors say that when in-law relations are strained or the subject matter

is difficult, it may be wiser to communicate through the bloodline. Do you agree or disagree? Why?

2. Read Hebrews 3:13 and Philippians 4:8. Why does Paul instruct us to think and speak positively about others? How would this practice improve relationships with in-laws?

3. Why is it important to relate to in-laws as friends rather than in a parent-child relationship?

4. Paul says we are to speak the truth in love (Eph 4:15). When something an in-law says or does bothers you, when do you think it is important to confront, and when do you think it is better to overlook?

5. Why is it important for couples to communicate a united front to their in-laws?

6. What principle or insight in this chapter was most helpful to you?

7
Pulling the Plug on Anger

A *young son-in-law shared an upsetting experience.* His family was vacationing at his in-laws', and his young children were playing in the driveway when his mother-in-law arrived home from grocery shopping. Before driving into the garage, she had to wait in her car a minute or more as he and his kids removed the kids' assorted toys from the driveway. As he helped her carry in the bags of groceries, it became obvious that his mother-in-law was irritated that she had had to wait—and that she'd had to buy so many groceries for her visiting family. When she suddenly barked at him, the son-in-law was unprepared for her anger and snapped back, "Don't yell at me, Mom." The sudden explosion from both parties caught them off guard, and it was several hours before the two of them were able to speak to each other again.

Principle Six: Become an Expert in Handling Your Anger

With good reason the apostle Paul instructs us, "Get rid of all bitterness, rage and anger, brawling and slander, along with every form of malice" (Eph 4:31). Mismanaged anger can destroy us and spell disaster in our relationship with our in-laws. If we lose our cool with our in-laws by venting our frustration in anger, it may be years before they will be able to forgive us. It's worth working on this area until we become experts in managing anger properly.

In Mark 3:1-5 we read the account of Jesus' healing a man's shriveled hand. The Pharisees were watching him closely to see if he would heal on the sabbath. Jesus was "deeply distressed at their stubborn hearts," and he "looked . . . at them in anger." He was justifiably angry that they cared more about their traditions than they did about people. Jesus' righteous anger gave birth to the finest teaching on hypocrisy the world has ever known.

The great American statesman Thomas Jefferson worked out a way to handle his anger, which he included in his "Rules of Living." He wrote: "When angry, count to ten before you speak; if very angry, a hundred." Mark Twain revised Jefferson's words about seventy-five years later: "When angry, count to four. When very angry, swear."[1] Haven't we all had moments when we were so upset we didn't know exactly how to vent our frustration?

Most Christians understand that walking with Christ involves seeking victory over external vices like drinking, pornography and profanity, yet many overlook the need to effectively deal with such things as anger, which can destroy us from within. The Holy Spirit longs to control all areas of our lives, inward as well as outward sins. Anger is one area we must relinquish to the Holy Spirit's control if we wish to successfully relate to our in-laws.

Anger itself is not wrong. It is a strong emotion of displeasure, usually in response to a frustrating or irritating situation. The emotion itself is not wrong, but what we choose to do with those angry feelings may be. The problem is that many of us have not learned to use that anger positively, and we vent our anger in harmful ways. "In your anger do not sin," the psalmist tells us (Ps 4:4). When we are angry, we can choose to use our anger to lead to a positive good or allow it to lead to sin.

Dealing Negatively with Anger

How should we deal with anger? There are three ways people commonly deal with anger, none of which is constructive. The first is *repression,* perhaps the worst way to manage anger. People who repress their anger deny they are angry. But that doesn't magically make it go away. Speaking at a conference, John Powell once said, "When I repress my emotions, my stomach keeps score." These people suffer from all kinds of physiological ailments as a result of their internalized anger. If you are repressing ill feelings toward your in-laws, you may be one of those whose body is paying the price.

One couple we know had one set of parents-in-law who were extremely negative people. Although the daughter-in-law would work hard in preparation for her in-laws' arrival, they never seemed to notice. When she received a special recognition at her part-time job, her mother-in-law's only comment was that she should be home with the kids. Although the daughter-in-law usually managed to put on a "happy face" during the visit in order to keep peace, every time the in-laws left she was sick with diarrhea for days.

Another way some deal with anger is through *suppression.* When in-laws suppress their anger, they often use underhanded or indirect methods of expressing it, such as pouting, gossip, sarcasm, criticism or bitterness. They may also keep you waiting, never return your phone calls, not answer your letters. If people don't deal directly with the resentment they have and instead respond sarcastically or bitterly, their anger can grow into deep-seated hatred.

We know of women who suppress so much anger toward their mothers-in-law that they have allowed it to spoil their relationship with their husbands. They begin to notice qualities in their husbands that remind them of their hated mothers-in-law and begin to pull back emotionally from their husbands. They allow a poor relationship with their in-laws to rub off on their marriages.

A third unproductive way people deal with anger is through *explosion*. Exploders are liable to fly off the handle without warning. They may respond to frustration by impaling tennis rackets on net posts or wrapping golf clubs around trees. They may express anger through desk pounding, face slapping, loud cussing, bitter putdowns or screaming.

One mother-in-law shocked her daughter-in-law by screaming at her, using an obscenity, without any warning—they weren't even having a dsagreement! The daughter-in-law was more than likely the recipient of unresolved anger in the mother-in-law's life, which probably took root years before the daughter-in-law became part of the family. Unresolved anger residing in an explosive personality usually does much harm to the target of the anger—and often to innocent bystanders as well.

There are many negative consequences of mismanaged anger toward our in-laws. We'd like to focus more closely on five.

1. Spiritual darkness. The Bible is clear: "Anyone who claims to be in the light but hates his brother is still in the darkness. Whoever loves his brother lives in the light, and there is nothing in him to make him stumble. But whoever hates his brother is in the darkness and walks around in the darkness; he does not know where he is going, because the darkness has blinded him" (1 Jn 2:9-11).

Have you ever gotten up in the middle of the night in a hotel room and couldn't find the light switch? You needed to answer the telephone or open a window, but instead you found yourself groping in inky blackness, bumping into the nightstand, banging your shin on a chair or tripping over your suitcase. Unresolved anger toward our in-laws can drive us into darkness, where we lose perspective and can't think logically. As we blindly stumble we don't realize what we're doing to ourselves and to those we love.

We pay the highest price for anger in the spiritual realm. Walking in the darkness of an angry spirit can destroy any desire we have for studying God's Word, praying or honoring Christ. That's why Paul writes, " 'In your anger do not sin': Do not let the sun go down while you are still angry, and do not give the devil a foothold" (Eph 4:26-27). When Satan gets a foothold in a person's life, the person is cast into a grim darkness. We know people who have allowed bitterness toward their in-laws to consume them and thereby damage their relationship with God. Peace has eluded them.

2. Damaged relationships. The social price paid for inner anger and bitterness is damaged relationships. If we hold on to angry feelings toward our in-laws, it will wreak havoc in our relationship with them. We read in 1 Samuel 20:30-33 that Saul's anger was kindled against his son Jonathan so much that he hurled his spear at him to kill him. So Jonathan fled from the palace. In the same way, unresolved anger toward in-laws will drive them away.

John Trent says that such anger "causes husbands and wives, parents and children and parents-in-law and children-in-law to drift away from each other. Homes become little more than dormitories with hostile roommates."[2] Family members may continue to coexist, but they're not close. In a marriage marred by anger, conversation may slacken and sexual expression may vanish. Anger can cause divorce or lead kids to run away from home. Injured in-laws learn to stay a safe distance away from angry family members to avoid further pain.

3. Damaged property. Several years ago we had some property at our house damaged due to anger. Ron was to take four of the boys to their tennis practice. When it was time to go, Ron stepped out of the study and announced that the boys were to report to the car. He found that none of them were ready, nor had they completed their jobs for the morning. Ron started to heat up. He yelled at them for not getting their work done and told them all to meet out at the car. Then he walked out to the car and waited. It was several minutes before the first boy came out of the house, half-dressed, racquet slung over his shoulder, carrying his shoes in his hand. The longer Ron waited, the angrier he became. How could they be so disorganized and ill-prepared?

By the time the last straggler dragged himself out of the house and crawled into the car, Ron was seething with anger. He stomped on the accelerator, assuming the car was in reverse. It wasn't! The car, in first gear, lurched forward, tearing a large hole in the garage door.

Ron shared this story from the pulpit on a Sunday morning. The congregation roared with laughter. The next week, several people told us they drove by our house after church, just to take a look at the garage! (But it wasn't funny the day it happened.)

Unbridled anger can have scary implications in in-law relationships too. Some people are so angry with their in-laws that they foolishly damage property and other possessions in their rage. After the damage has been done, it's too late for regrets.

4. Illness. Mismanaged anger can also cause illness. Anger, like few other emotions, can restrict and bind us and tie us in internal knots. Our bodies can pay a big price. One psychologist estimates that as many as 97 percent of the people who come to him with ulcers have them because of anger.[3] When your body is stimulated by anger, your whole musculature grows rigid, which can lead to headaches, colitis, back-aches or hypertension. Unresolved conflict between in-laws can cause people to be physically ill. When people say their in-laws make them sick, they may not be kidding!

5. Infection of others. One last sad consequence of anger is that it spreads to and infects family members, friends and coworkers. Solomon tells us, "Do not make friends with a hot-tempered man, do not associate with one easily angered, or you may learn his ways and get yourself ensnared" (Prov 22:24-25). Studies of people convicted of violent crimes indicate that most violent criminals learned from one or more violent role models. If you are reaping a crop of anger in your relationship with your in-laws, investigation may reveal that you have been sowing a crop of anger and bitterness among others.

Overcoming Destructive Anger

How can destructive anger be overcome? If you carry feelings of anger toward a parent-in-law or child-in-law and often feel that you're held hostage by your own anger, the good news is that your expression of anger can come under your control. You're not at the mercy of your feelings; you're in the driver's seat and can direct your actions. You can learn to handle that anger. We'd like to offer twelve practical suggestions for how this can be done.

1. Recognize that negative results outweigh the positive. The reason many people become addicted to anger is because it seems to get results. If you vent your frustration at an in-law for doing something that irritates you, the odds are good that he or she won't repeat the action. Most people are frightened by an explosion of anger, so it appears that the anger is effective in inciting change. But in the long run, yelling usually produces negative results.

We're not usually looking for terrified obedience; we're looking for people who appreciate our thoughts and feelings, who are sensitive to our needs and love us. The "target" of an angry tirade is more likely to be filled with resentment and disrespect than love for us. So the relief we feel after an angry outburst is hollow and short-lived, and the relationship will probably worsen rather than improve. Long-term negative results of yelling, screaming and pounding substantially outweigh the positive results. Anger just doesn't achieve what we think it will.

2. Resolve to learn self-control. "Like a city whose walls are broken down is a man who lacks self-control" (Prov 25:28). When we lack self-control, we are vulnerable and defenseless against the power of anger. Galatians tells us that one fruit of the Spirit is self-control (5:22-23). We should pray that we might have the Spirit's self-control.

If we want to learn self-control, we must ask ourselves questions like "When I am angry with my in-law, do I wish I was in full control of my behavior? If I want to be in full control of myself when I am with my in-laws, am I willing to spend the energy required to learn self-control?" When we feel ourselves starting to lose control of our anger, it would be wise to ask ourselves, "Is this really the way I want to act around my in-laws?"

3. Memorize Scripture. Wrong behavior emanates from wrong thinking. The best way to get rid of wrong thinking is to replace it with right thinking. This is where Scripture memorization can be helpful. The Bible has much to say about patience and self-control: "A fool shows his annoyance at once, but a prudent man overlooks an insult. . . . A patient man has great understanding, but a quick-tempered man displays folly. . . . Better a patient man than a warrior, a man who controls his temper than one who takes a city" (Prov 12:16; 14:29; 16:32).

God says that when we are wildly out of control with anger, we show ourselves to be fools. Is that what we want to be? We certainly don't want our in-laws to call us fools. Isn't it better to be a patient person who shows wisdom? Reading and memorizing Scripture helps us replace old habits of dealing with frustration with more godly, healthy habits.

4. Confess anger and the need for God's help. We must understand that all anger is ultimately expressed to God. When David committed adultery with Bathsheba and had her husband murdered, he eventually confessed to God, "Against you, you only, have I sinned" (Ps 51:4). If we believe God is sovereign, we realize all anger is ultimately directed to him.

If we harbor feelings of resentment toward our in-laws, we cannot overcome our bitterness on our own strength. We need to ask Christ to help us, to change us and give us his nature. We need God each moment of the day to help us be who he wants us to be. That's what Paul discovered when he wrote, "Not that we are competent in ourselves to claim anything for ourselves, but our competence comes from God" (2 Cor 3:5).

5. Delay your responses. In James 1:19 we read, "My dear brothers, take note of this: Everyone should be quick to listen, slow to speak and slow to become angry." We are admonished to be slow to anger. This means we need to get ahead of our behavior and think before we explode and say something we will later regret. Practically speaking, if we find ourselves in a discussion with an in-law and it begins heating up, we need to learn to back off. Doing so can give us time to think about what is happening, why we are getting upset, and how we want to handle the situation.

6. Let go of your anger quickly. The apostle Paul says, " 'In your anger, do not sin': Do not let the sun go down while you are still angry, and do not give the devil a foothold" (Eph 4:26-27). We notice from these verses that it's okay to feel anger. But it's not okay to allow it to turn into bitterness. We are exhorted not to *stay* angry. Rather, we are encouraged to get rid of anger quickly—even before bedtime.

The story is told of Robert E. Lee visiting a woman who had lost a husband and a son in the Civil War. She pointed to the charred remains of a big oak tree that had burned in her front yard. She said, "See that tree? It represents my bitterness, my anger about the war. I have left it there to remind me of my resentment." General Lee said to her, "Cut it down. Cut it down."

In a similar way, if a root of bitterness has grown in your life toward an in-law, it is wise to cut it down. Get rid of it as quickly as possible.

When we sold our first home, we accepted an offer with certain conditions and restrictions. One condition was that we were to leave a refrigerator in good working order. About three months after we had moved, we received a phone call from our buyer. He told us the refrigerator had quit working. He wanted a new one, in fact, a new one three times the price of the model we had left. We said we didn't think we owed him anything more. In anger he said, "Okay, I'll see you in court!" and he hung up. Jorie and I felt we didn't owe him more, since we had been generous with him in the price of the home and cooperated one-hundred percent with all of the conditions in the agreement. And the refrigerator had been working fine when we left.

Still, we did not want to tarnish Christ's name and certainly did not want to take a trip to court, so we called him back and made a compromise offer. Our peace offering was accepted. Was he right and were we wrong? No. Did we owe him anything? Probably not. But was it worth it to us to make peace with him? Yes. Many times it's worth it to be the generous one and to offer the peace pipe.

Many times, however—maybe particularly with our in-laws—we may fail to heed Christ's call for immediate action. Instead of being generous, we choose to fight, squabble or cling to bitterness rather than reconcile. Yet if we do not move toward reconciliation quickly, the damage can be incalculable. If you've wronged your son- or daughter-in-law or mother- or father-in-law and don't move quickly to reconcile, things are only going to get worse! If an in-law has hurt you and you do not let go of your anger but instead allow bitterness to fester within you, you are headed for trouble. It may be that you have been grossly wronged by an in-law, but when someone wrongs you, it's your responsibility to make sure you don't hang on to bitterness, or you're wrong too.

Romans 12:19 helps us. "Do not take revenge, my friends, but leave room for God's wrath, for it is written: 'It is mine to avenge; I will repay,' says the Lord." If we have been treated unfairly by our in-laws, our natural reaction may be to try to get back at them. But if we remember it's not our job to set the record straight, we can let go of our anger and trust that God will make all things right someday.

7. Cultivate healthy self-esteem. As we discussed in chapter three, healthy self-esteem is vital to loving in-laws. It is also important in curbing anger in our in-law relationships. Anger and low self-esteem are often closely linked. Affronts to our self-esteem through insults or humiliation are perhaps the most powerful elicitors of anger.

In addition, persons with poor self-esteem can become angry as a result of feeling threatened by other people. A mother-in-law who has poor self-esteem may feel angry if her son pays more attention to her daughter-in-law than to her. If we maintain a healthy self-concept, fewer experiences will hurt or threaten us. When an in-law criticizes us, it will not incite our anger by threatening our self-concept, for we know we are made in God's image and have infinite value.

8. Stay in close touch with your feelings. When you are angry, it is almost always because you are experiencing some form of pain. You may become angry because an expectation has gone unfulfilled. You wanted your parents-in-law to come for your baby's baptism and they declined, choosing to go out of town for the weekend instead. Or your son-in-law chooses another insurance agent instead of allowing you to write the policies for your daughter's family. If you want to short-circuit anger, you need to get in touch with your feelings by asking yourself, "Why am I angry? What goal or desire is being frustrated? What needs do I have which I think this other person is failing to meet?" If you can determine why you are heating up, you can take steps to keep yourself under control.

Keeping a journal helps us stay in touch with our feelings. Writing why we get angry helps us understand ourselves so we are less likely to lose our cool when a similar situation arises. If you struggle with anger toward your in-laws, try keeping a record in each case of why you became angry.

One day, when one of our boys was eight, I reprimanded him. He ran out of the room very upset. Five minutes later he brought this note to me:

Dear Dad,

I'm leaving for Sunriver, Oregon. I will be back in 8 years.

Your angry friend, _____

Through the years, writing has been a great way for this boy to vent his feelings. Another time when he was upset with me, he taped this note on his door:

STAY OUT! ANGRY BEAST INSIDE THIS ROOM!

These expressions are healthy. Telling God your feelings is also healthy. If we tell God when we are upset, it helps us not explode at other people. One of our friends writes down all of the things her mother and mother-in-law do that make her angry and all of the things they do that make her happy. She does this so she won't forget how she is feeling now. Then, when she becomes a mother-in-law someday, she will remember the practical wisdom she experienced as a daughter-in-law and be able to use it to help her be a wise mother-in-law. We know she will be.

9. Express your feelings only when it helps you minister to the person. You may wonder, "When is it okay to vent my feelings of frustration with another person?" Couples often ask, "Should we tell each other everything we feel? Should we always tell each other when we are angry? When something the in-laws have done is upsetting to us, should we tell them?"

When we experience feelings of anger, we may feel as if only two options are open to us: (1) we can stuff our feelings inside, or (2) we can assertively dump them on others. The problem with repressing our feelings is that we haven't taken care of our anger; we've only masked it, and often it surfaces later in damaging ways. On the other hand, the trouble with venting our anger is that it tends to encourage even more aggressive behavior.

There is another option. Ezekiel writes:

The word of the LORD came to me: "Son of man, with one blow I am about to take away from you the delight of your eyes. Yet do not lament or weep or shed any tears. Groan quietly; do not mourn for the dead." (Ezek 24:15-17)

The death of Ezekiel's wife was an occasion for profound grief. But notice how God instructed Ezekiel to handle his feelings. God told him to "groan quietly." God authenticated his feelings and let him know that his feelings weren't wrong. He was instructed to acknowledge them. God also instructed him to deny himself any form of public expression of his private grief. Ezekiel was to acknowledge inwardly how he felt, but he was not to express this outwardly.

In this instance, God had a definite reason why he didn't want Ezekiel to share his feelings openly. The unique absence of mourning was, in this case, intended to convey that the impending judgment for Judah's sin would be so severe that, by comparison, the death of a wife warranted no tears at all. In this case, public expression of his feelings did not fit God's purpose.

When something your mother- or father-in-law or son- or daughter-in-law has said or done is upsetting to you and anger arises within you, acknowledge to yourself and to God how you feel. But this doesn't necessarily give you license to dump your feelings on him or her. You may need to subordinate the public expression of your feelings to your desire to allow God to use you for his purposes. You should express your feelings to the person only when you sense that it would further God's purpose of ministry to them. If not, then it may be wise to drop the matter.

Yes, it is a scriptural principle that if your brother offends you, you should go to him, but here is an additional principle which must be considered. For example, it might feel humiliating to a parent-in-law to be confronted by his or her daughter- or son-in-law, who may be half his or her age. In this case it may be best to remain silent if sharing our feelings would further damage a struggling relationship. Maybe exercising self-control and loving our in-laws enough that we won't embarrass them is a more godly act than confronting them with the truth. This is neither stuffing nor venting our feelings but choosing to channel them in a mature way—telling our feelings to God but not sharing them publicly.

10. Seek reconciliation. When you've hurt someone by an expression of anger or someone has hurt you, Jesus says to seek reconciliation as soon as possible:

> Therefore, if you are offering your gift at the altar and there remember that your brother has something against you, leave your gift there in front of the altar. First go and be reconciled to your brother; then come and offer your gift (Mt 5:23-24).

Several steps help untie the knots of anger in the process of reconciliation.

First, *become soft and tender.* Solomon writes, "A gentle answer turns away wrath, but a harsh word stirs up anger" (Prov 15:1). Our family is learning that when one family member snipes at another, an argument can be avoided if the other person responds with a gentle answer. When we speak kindly, our words are like pouring oil on troubled waters.

Second, *admit you were wrong.* The toughest words we will ever have to say to an in-law will be "I was wrong." Jim Brauner did a survey of several thousand high-school students at his summer camp. He found the number-one complaint teenagers voiced about their parents could be summed up in five words: "They never say 'I'm sorry.' " They don't admit they're wrong.[5]

In admitting we're wrong, we need to be careful not to settle for the cheap substitute. This cheapening of an apology involves adding the little word *if*. It goes like this. "If I was wrong, please forgive me." "If I hurt you, I want you to know I'm so sorry." The problem with "if" is it spoils the whole statement. With "if" included, there is no admission of guilt. What the person is saying is, "I don't think I was wrong, but if *you* do, then I'm sorry." "I don't think I was wrong, but since obviously *you* do (you're really the one who has a problem, not me), then I'm sorry." If you and I want a restored relationship, we must humble ourselves and admit we were wrong. Often it's not easy to admit to an in-law that we were wrong, but it's amazing how smoldering angry relationships can begin to be repaired when we do.

Third, *ask forgiveness and wait for a response.* Say, "I'm sorry. What I did wasn't what Jesus would do. Would you . . . could you forgive me?" Then wait for the response.

Fourth, *promise to never do it again.* Proverbs 28:13 says: "He who conceals his sins does not prosper, but whoever confesses and renounces them finds mercy." True confession involves repentance, a commitment to never do it again.

A number of times I have come to Jorie and said, "I'm sorry, will you forgive me?" And she has said, "No, I won't forgive you. You're just going to do it again." And you know, she's right! If we don't commit to change, our confession is hollow.

Fifth, *make restitution.* Suppose you drive to church in a brand-new BMW. You've got that baby all shined up and you're pleased as punch.

After church I get in my tiny Subaru Justy. It's got a number of years on it. It didn't cost me much to begin with, and it's never had a wax job, so I'm not too worried about it. Consequently, I carelessly wheel out of my parking spot and *wham,* I put a serious crease along the side of your car. It looks a mess.

I say to you, "Boy, I'm really sorry, but I'm sure thankful for God's grace, aren't you? I asked God to forgive me and I feel better already. Have a nice day." That just wouldn't cut it. Apologies without restitution won't do. If you've wronged an in-law, you will need to make restitution, if at all possible.

11. Slacken your stride. One-quarter of Americans today say they're simply exhausted. Explosions of anger are far more likely to occur when we're constantly running at breakneck speed. If we miss one section of a revolving door, we're thrown into a tizzy fit. By lightening our schedules and taking lots of minute vacations each day to praise God and relax, we can greatly reduce the likelihood of uncontrolled anger. Once, for several weeks, I kept a record of all the times I got angry. I found that three-fourths of my outbursts were related to being late and trying to pack too much into a day. If you and I want to avoid run-ins with our in-laws, it may help us to take some of the hurry out of our lives and schedule more time for building our relationships with our in-laws.

12. Transfer your rights to God. If you take time to carefully study the times you get angry, you'll probably find that practically all of it involves a violation of what you consider a personal right. The apostle Paul writes: "I have been crucified with Christ and I no longer live, but Christ lives in me. The life I live in the body, I live by faith in the Son of God, who loved me and gave himself for me" (Gal 2:20). When we embrace Christ, we tell him we want to die to ourselves and come alive to what he wants us to do. If we want to beat anger toward our in-laws, we need to seriously consider transferring our rights to God. How do we do this?

We can start by praying, "God, I give up my rights. I want only what you want for me. I give up my right to a warm welcome when I visit my in-laws. I give up the right to a mother-in-law who treats me with respect or a daughter-in-law who adores me. Instead, I'll let you call the shots, and I'll be thankful for whatever you choose to give me."

If we are willing to give up our personal rights, we may be pleasantly surprised to discover our anger dissipating as well. If we have fewer rights which can be violated, we'll find we may get angry far less often.

Thank God that anger does not have to prevail. If your relationship with your mother-, father-, son-, daughter-, brother- or sister-in-law has been injured by anger, seek reconciliation. Pull the plug on anger. Ask the person to forgive you. Forgive him or her too (even if he or she doesn't ask). Experience the reality that anger can be overcome and relationships can heal.

Questions for Reflection or Discussion

1. Define and contrast the three ways people commonly deal with anger: *repression, suppression* and *explosion.*

2. Read 1 John 2:9-11 and Ephesians 4:26-27. Describe how and why anger pushes us into spiritual darkness.

3. Read Proverbs 22:24-25. How might anger spread from one family member to another or from one in-law to another?

4. The authors say that the long-term negative results of anger far outweigh the positive. Do you agree or disagree? Why?

5. Memorize one or more of the following verses: Proverbs 12:16; 14:29; 16:32; 22:24-25; Ephesians 4:26-27. Share with a friend or fellow group member why these verses are meaningful to you.

6. How do you know when sharing your feelings of anger will help you minister to your in-laws?

7. Of the five steps identified for seeking reconciliation, which ones are most frequently overlooked?

8. What principle or insight in this chapter was most helpful to you?

8
Grandparenting

G*od has blessed our church with a* fine pastoral staff. When I began pastoring here in 1981, I was the only pastor, for we had only a handful of people. As God has added people to our congregation, we have had to add staff. One of the first people we added was a fellow Presbyterian pastor to work with our adult ministries. Today he is our senior associate pastor who oversees most of the staff.

His children are a few years older than ours, so we have had the opportunity of watching him up close as his children married and he officiated at their weddings. I sensed a bit of sadness in him as his kids married, moved away and left him with an empty nest. But then his first grandchild was born. He was so excited. He was like a little kid in a candy store. He loves to visit his grandchildren and talks about them frequently. He has shown us what a thrill grandparenting can be.

Principle Seven: Grandparents Fulfill a Huge Need When They Assume the Role of Nurturers

Unfortunately, one of the areas which can cause tension with in-laws is disagreement over parenting styles and the role of grandparents. What part do grandparents play in the home? How important are they to the family structure? What does the Bible have to say about grandparents? How can we relieve in-law tensions in the area of grandparenting? If approached sensitively, in-law problems in the area of grandparenting can be avoided and grandparenting can be a fulfilling experience for all involved. We would like to offer the following suggestions which, if put into practice, may help your family minimize tensions that have divided many of the best families. Keep in mind that each family is unique, and each suggestion will be more appropriate to some family situations than to others.

Offer to Help

In accordance with your time and energy, offer to help with your grand-children. Children today have many needs—emotional, mental, social, physical and spiritual. And meeting all of them places a stressful demand on parents. Some grandparents have discovered that they want to share some of the responsibilities, and from their perspective, gain a great feeling of self-worth. Parents and parents-in-law who enjoy helping with their grandchildren and who have the physical health and time to invest can make the load less heavy for their adult children.

But let the parents call the shots; ask in what ways you can be of most help. They are the ones with the main responsibility for raising these children. You are offering to support their program, not to compete.

If you volunteer to spend time with the grandchildren, you will be less likely to feel used or imposed upon than if the parents had to ask for your help. And you are then free to set the parameters on when and for how long you will spend time with the kids.

Anything you do for your grandchildren can help. For example, when our parents are in town visiting us, we find it a big help when they take special time to read to some of the kids before bed. It's a help to us and the kids love it. (Reading time usually lasts longer when Grandma or Grandpa are doing the reading.)

In Psalm 128 we read, "May the LORD bless you from Zion all the days of your life; may you see the prosperity of Jerusalem, and may you live to see your children's children. Peace be upon Israel" (vv. 5-6). Living to see our grandchildren is considered a blessing from God. Grandparents who are able to spend time with their grandchildren participate in a triple blessing. These grandparents are able to have influence in their grandchildren's lives, which is very fulfilling; grandchildren have a special opportunity to experience the special love, care and wisdom a grandparent can uniquely offer; and the married children will receive a welcome break.

Many grandparents have commented that the nice thing about grandparenting is that the grandkids are not their ultimate responsibility. One grandparent cleverly captured the feeling on paper:

I've seen the lights of Paris,
I've seen the lights of Rome,
But the lights that excite me most are the
Taillights on my children's car
Driving the grandchildren home.

Grandparents who desire to spend time with their grandchildren are most likely to find the freedom to do so if they observe a few practical do's and don'ts in the process:

1. Never criticize your children's parenting efforts or offer suggestions without being asked. T. Berry Brazelton tells of when his daughter and her husband brought their newborn to visit them for the first time. The baby was fussy and turbulent. The new parents hovered over her, picking her up to feed every hour. His daughter was exhausted. Now, Dr. Brazelton was a pediatrician, so you can imagine he had some strong opinions! In retrospect, he says he made the mistake of giving them advice too soon. He suggested they allow the baby to work out some of her difficulties for herself by letting her fuss for a few minutes before going to her.

"Don't rush to feed her every hour," he advised his daughter, "or your milk won't keep coming in."

"You don't know our baby," his son-in-law broke in quickly.

He was right. Dr. Brazelton realized he had stepped in too soon, ignoring the new parents' efforts to learn about their child. He waited and watched for a while and grew to respect their anxious handling of their daughter as a sign of their intense caring. A week later, when he did know her, they were able to discuss the baby together, and then his daughter and son-in-law were open to some of his suggestions.

Dr. Brazelton learned a great deal from that episode—primarily that his granddaughter was his *children's* baby, and it was vital that he acknowledge that. When he as a grandfather stepped in too soon, it shook the young parents' confidence at a time when they needed to feel they alone were in control. His advice to other grandparents? Grandparents are vital as supports, not as critics.[1]

Being a parent is difficult. It's even harder if there's a mother- or father-in-law watching and waiting for you to mess up. One young mom shared her frustration after her mother-in-law kept her three-year-old son for the weekend. When she picked him up, she found her mother-in-law had washed and ironed all of his clothes, including underwear and T-shirts. And she had written out instructions on how to wash her grandson's clothes, including details such as "turn clothes inside out before placing in the washing machine." This mom wanted to turn her *mother-in-law* inside out.[2]

Criticism falls flat in grandparenting. Just as grandparents are wise to be supportive rather than critical of their children's parenting style, they are wise to make it their policy to never criticize their grandchildren. Most criticism of grandchildren is received as a reflection on the parents, so it will most likely drive a wedge between you and your adult child and son- or daughter-in-law. Rather, it is wise for grandparents to enjoy their grandchildren instead of evaluating them.

With all the years of hard-earned wisdom grandparents possess, it takes much love, patience and self-control to hold their tongues and watch their children make mistakes in child-rearing. The self-control needed here is similar to that which we need when we teach our children to take their first steps, to ride two-wheelers and to drive. It's nerve-wracking to watch our baby fall, or to let go of a wobbly bike, or to sit silently on the passenger side while the car careens across the center line. But just as our children learn from mistakes when they are young, they will learn to become good parents through some trial and error. They need our praise just as much as adults as they did as children—perhaps more. Some parents and parents-in-law forget this principle when their children become adults. Wise parents and parents-in-law will continue to affirm their children, especially in this tender area of parenting.

On the other hand, wise sons and daughters, sons- and daughters-in-law will seek the counsel of their parents and parents-in-law, asking questions in areas where they need advice. Asking questions gives parents and parents-in-law an opportunity to share their wisdom without feeling they're interfering.

2. Never criticize your children or offer suggestions in front of your grandchildren. This practice can undermine their parental authority and may likely put them on the defensive. It's wiser to give advice only when you and your child are alone. In like manner, children and children-in-law should give the same consideration to their parents and parents-in-law, and they should make sure any admonishing is done privately, never in front of the children.

In *Then God Created Grandparents,* Charlie Shedd shares one grand-mother's testimony:

> See my red hair! I'm the kind who likes to say what I think and it hasn't always been so good. But I want you to know I've learned most of the time with my grandchildren it's better I keep my big mouth shut.[3]

That's not bad advice. We know that both our sets of parents would have chosen to do some things differently with our children than we have chosen to do, but both have usually worked hard to not offer advice unless it is solicited. We appreciate that.

3. Never interfere with your children's discipline of their children. If you can't stand watching how your children are handling a situation with the grandchildren, perhaps it's best that you go for a walk. Maybe the parents are wrong. But interfering will probably only make it worse. We know many grandparents struggle with this problem. When they see their children making discipline mistakes, they so badly want to help them avoid these parenting pitfalls. Everything within them may scream to step in and intercede on behalf of the grandchildren, but they are wise to bite their tongues and stay out of it. The only possible exception to this rule might be in cases when the children are being physically or emotionally abused.

4. Never discipline grandchildren when the parents are around. It is most wise for grandparents to let their children handle all discipline of the grandchildren. Discipline is not usually the responsibility of the grandparents. To offer discipline advice is usually overstepping your bounds. Your interference communicates a lack of confidence in your children, which will very likely drive a wedge between you and your son or son-in-law and daughter or daughter-in-law.

Consequently, when grandparents are taking care of the grandchildren, they must be authorized by the children's parents to use discipline. It is wise to discuss and agree with your children ahead of time concerning the disciplinary methods you may use when you are alone with the grandchildren. Whether it be spanking, time-outs or withholding rewards, grandparents are wise to seek clear direction on how they may discipline the grandchildren. Since this role is the parents' God-given responsibility, it is wise for all families to understand that even if they are in the grandparents' home, the children are the parents' responsibility and, therefore, the role of discipline still belongs to the parents.

Does this mean a grandparent must tolerate pillow fights or jumping on living room couches or watch in horror while toddlers play with valuable figurines? Absolutely not. If grandchildren are visiting a grandparents' home, the home is the responsibility of the grandparents. Thus if grandchildren are not respecting property in the way in which the grandparents are comfortable, the grandparents should set the parameters. For example, statements such as, "Jessica, in Grandma and Grandpa's house it's not okay to pick all the roses," or "Conner, if your mommy lets you jump on your bed at home, that's fine, but at Grandma's house pillows are only for sleeping," or "Abby, these treasures in Grandma and Grandpa's house are just to look at, not to touch." All the above issues have to do with the grandparents' property and are, consequently, most appropriate for grandparent-set rules. However, issues like giving children treats, setting bedtimes or disciplining are child-related issues which should have the parents' input. Considerate sons- and daughters-in-law and sons and daughters will ask their parents and parents-in-law what special consideration needs to be taken while visiting their homes, and they will help enforce that behavior in their children.

5. *Respect your children's decisions.* Where they live, what they buy, how many children they have, where they go on vacations and how they raise their children are *their* decisions. Parents have approximately eighteen years to pass values on to their children. When the children leave home to establish families of their own, they will be responsible for their own decisions. One young man wrote to his in-laws concerning this area of responsibility:

The one thing I ask of you is to please make an effort to follow my wishes regarding discipline with the grandchildren. For example, as we both know, you used to allow them to eat while watching the television in the family room while I preferred for them to eat at the table. The last time we visited your home, I was pleased to notice you never fed them in front of the television. I appreciate your responsiveness.

However, I am still concerned that our kids get a little spoiled with you. For example, we have been trying to teach them that they need to eat what they are served. I noticed that at your home if they were served what everyone else was eating and they said they didn't like it, you would ask them what they want and prepare them a different meal. Even after I mentioned to you my concern, you still catered to their desires.

One of the rules in our home is that the kids have to eat all their dinner if they are to be candidates for dessert. They aren't required to eat everything that is served, but if they want to have dessert, they must eat everything on their plate. We have found that dessert is highly motivating to our children, so we seldom have family members who do not finish their dinner.

For a period of time, we had trouble enforcing this rule when we traveled to my parents' home. The kids' indulgent grandmother did not expect them to finish their dinner to qualify for having dessert. She told the kids that when they were at Grandma's house they could have dessert without finishing the rest of their food. Yes, she had a right to have different rules in her home, but they were still our children, and we had no intention of changing our rules just because we were not in our own house. So I spoke to my mom about this issue one night, and we've never had a problem over this subject again. She has respected our decision regarding desserts.

Perhaps young parents could overlook some of their parents' and in-laws' unintentional interference with the grandchildren if they understood the place grandchildren play in most grandparents' hearts. The love grandparents feel for their children's wee little ones sometimes is overwhelming. One grandmother told us she and her husband were unprepared for the depth of emotion and sense of responsibility their granddaughter brought to their lives. She has asked her daughter-in-law several times to tell her if she is stepping out of bounds, and her son has had a way of gently saying "Yes, mother," that lets her know when to back off. When children understand how much their parents love their kids, it helps them be more forgiving of their occasional overprotectiveness or excessive indulgence toward the grandchildren.

Wise children also learn to separate the relationship they have with their parents and in-laws as their own parents from the relationship they have with them in their role as grandparents and grandparents-in-law. It would be wonderful if all these complex in-law relationships were strong ones. But this is not always the case. It is possible for a woman to be a tremendous mother and mother-in-law but not a particularly attentive grandmother. Or a man may be a fun-loving and attentive grandfather but not an especially pleasant father or father-in-law. All of us have roles in which we are stronger and weaker, and we need to allow family members the freedom to be who they are and to focus on their strengths, allowing them to grow in other areas.

Not all parents and parents-in-law want to or are able to baby-sit for their grandchildren, and it is unfair for children and children-in-law to expect them to. We know of children and children-in-law who have allowed themselves to become bitter towards their parents and in-laws because they expect them to help out with child care—and the grandparents don't or can't. This expectation toward the parents and in-laws is wrong, and the accompanying resentment is both wrong and hurtful. Grandparents do not owe their children baby-sitting. Mature children and children-in-law will understand this fact and protect the relationship they have with their parents and parents-in-law by not placing unfair pressure on them regarding child care. The truth is parents can be great parents and in-laws—and terrific grandparents and grandparents-in-law—even if they never baby-sit. Give them that chance.

Assume the Role of a Nurturer

One of the most important roles grandparents can assume, if they are interested, is that of nurturer with their grandchildren. Rather than assuming the role of parent or disciplinarian, God has designed grandparents to fill the important role of nurturer. Since grandparents are not usually caught up in the daily, practical tasks of raising children, they can focus on other areas. For example, grandparents can share with their grandchildren stories about their own lives, which is something parents often are too busy to do. Maybe the grandparents were the last ones chosen for the baseball team, and that knowledge might make a big difference to a child who barely made the team.

Grandparents don't usually have to ask pin-you-to-the-wall questions like "Did you brush your teeth?" or "Have you finished your homework?" or "Isn't it your turn to do the dishes?" or "Did you make your bed?" Instead, grandparents can ask questions like "What would you like to do tonight?" Usually they can afford the time to play. What a gift that is to children with extra-busy parents.

While many parents are just too tired and busy to take time to split an ice-cream sundae with their children, many grandparents delight in spending one-on-one time with their grandchildren. For grandparents with a somewhat more relaxed schedule, getting somewhere on time may not be half as important as enjoying the trip. Grandparents who have the time to invest can play a huge role in cultivating the self-esteem of their grandchildren. One grandchild identified this nurturing role of grandparents when she said, "Grandparents let you do things all by yourself, even if it takes longer and doesn't look too good."

A third grader was asked to write a theme for school on "What Is a Grandma?" She wrote:

A grandma is a lady who has no children of her own, so she likes other people's little girls. A grandpa is a man grandma. He goes for walks with boys and talks about fishing and stuff. Grandmas don't have anything to do except be there. Grandmas drive you to the supermarket where the pretend horse is and they have lots of dimes ready. Or if they take you for walks, they slow down past pretty leaves and caterpillars. Grandmas never say "Hurry up." Sometimes grandmas are fat but not too fat to tie kids' shoes. Grandmas wear glasses. And they can take their teeth and gums off. They answer questions like "Why do dogs hate cats?" and "How come God isn't married?" When they read to us, they don't skip words or mind if it's the same story again. Everybody should try to have a grandma, especially if you don't have a TV because grandmas are the only grown-ups who have got time.[4]

The gift of time is one of the most precious possessions grandparents can offer their grandchildren. Our kids love it each time our parents come to our home or we travel to see them because they love the time the grandparents take for them. Board and card games are not something Jorie and I play a lot with our kids. Neither do we take time for jigsaw puzzles. But our kids know they can always talk Grandma or Grandpa into a game or two, or a walk or a talk.

It is possible for grandparents to nurture their grandchildren even when they do not live nearby or see them often. Extended families usually don't live in the same town or in the same house as they used to. In addition, many grandparents move away from their families to warm places like Florida or Arizona to retire. Others move to age-segregated communities, which may mean they do not live close to grandchildren. Parents, too, pack up their families and move away from the grandparents because of a better job or a better environment in which to raise children.

Even in these situations, grandparents need not be strangers to their grandchildren. In these cases, bonding requires more creativity. Grandparents can build significant relationships with their grandchildren through letters and phone calls. Our kids have always loved to talk to their grandparents on the phone and are really excited to get letters from them. When our kids were in grade school and learning to write, it was great fun to exchange letters with Grandma and Grandpa. When the grandparents noticed that several of our kids were artistically inclined, they encouraged them to mail them pieces of their artwork, which they proudly displayed on their refrigerators.

Throughout history, grandparents have helped parents with the task of raising children. We can't forget that when the grandparents are not there, the parents wind up with a larger load to handle by themselves. Grandparents who live far away from children and grandchildren can endear themselves to their adult children and children-in-law by sending notes saying, "You sure are doing a great job as parents!" Looking for ways to encourage our families, even from far away, always helps to build our relationship with our in-laws.

Sensitive children and children-in-law will bridge the distance between grandparents and grandchildren by enabling their children to build strong relationships with their grandparents. Sending grandparents calendars of grandchildren's major events or inviting them to come for a play or swim meet may help grandparents feel more a part of their grandchildren's lives. Thoughtful children will make sure the grandchildren remember their grandparents on special days.

In Proverbs 17:6 Solomon writes: "Children's children are a crown to the aged, and parents are the pride of their children." Grandchildren are a delight to grandparents. And grandchildren are proud of their grandparents. They are good for each other. That's God's plan. One thing is for certain: when grandchildren are present, there ought to be lots of laughs. After a Christmas break, a teacher asked her pupils how they spent their holiday. Here is one young boy's reply:

We always spend Christmas with Grandma and Grandpa. They used to live up here in a big brick house but they got retarded and they moved to Florida. They live in a place with a lot of retarded people. They live in tin huts and ride big three-wheel tricycles. They got a big building they call a "wreck hall," but if it wrecked, it is fixed now. They play games and do exercises, but they don't do them very good. There is a swimming pool and they go to it and just stand there in the water with their hats on. I guess they don't know how to swim. My Grandma used to bake a lot of cookies and stuff, but I guess she forgot how. Nobody cooks there; they all go to fast-food restaurants. As you come into the park, there is a doll house with a man sitting in it. He watches all day so they can't get out without him seeing them. They wear badges with their names on them. I guess they don't know who they are. My Grandma says Grandpa worked hard all his life and earned his retardment. I wish they would move back home. But I guess the man in the doll house won't let them out.[5]

Enjoying a lot of laughs and good times with grandchildren has to be one of the greatest joys of retirement.

Jack Hayford tells of his four-year-old granddaughter coming to him one day. Jack asked her, "What do you want to be when you grow up?"

"I want to be a princess and a grandmother."

"Oh? And what do princesses do?"

"Princesses put on pretty dresses and dance around you."

"Oh, and what do grandmothers do?"

"Grandmothers wash dishes, sweep the floor, make the beds."

Then she added, "I think I'll just be a princess."

Grandparents can play an especially important role in nurturing grandchildren when a major change has occurred in the family due to divorce, separation, illness or death. Regardless of what circumstances may have occurred or how complicated things have become, your grandchildren will still need you. And you need them. In a time of storm, grandparents can be an anchor for them. Mature children will encourage grandparents to spend time with their children during stormy times in their own relationships, realizing they can be a stabilizing influence.

Seek Permission Before Giving Gifts

Often, grandparents have the means to be of tremendous assistance to their children financially. They may be able to help with summer camps, private lessons, orthodontics or college tuition. They can make things possible for their grandchildren that otherwise might be out of the question. Parents with little cash for extras may appreciate their help. But grandparents who are wise exercise caution with their gifts. They must be careful never to try to buy their grandchildren's love. They should take special care to never give something to the grandchildren that the parents do not want them to have.

If grandparents persist in giving a gift the parents have forbidden, they are in danger of driving a deep wedge between themselves and their children. Parents and parents-in-law who want to have good relationships with their children and children-in-law will ask about the appropriateness of a gift before giving it. Our parents have been generous with our children—and they have always asked us before giving large gifts.

Wise grandparents also will be careful that gifts will not give the impression of playing favorites. If the oldest grandchild receives a check for graduation or some other accomplishment, grandparents should try their best to remember to do something similar for the other youngsters when they reach their goals. Some grandparents have found that keeping written records helps them remember gifts so they can be sure to treat other grandchildren in similar ways.

Grandchildren do not need to be treated identically, for they are all different with different interests and needs, but care needs to be taken so that one child does not feel cheated or ignored. Sometimes an older child receives a gift that can't be given to younger siblings because the finances of grandparents have changed, and these situations should be treated with understanding and sensitivity. Wise children and children-in-law will treat gifts from parents and parents-in-law as exactly that— gifts—and should never have expectations regarding what they or their children should or should not be receiving from the grandparents. Grandparents have no *obligation* to their grandchildren.

Pass On a Spiritual Legacy
When all is said and done, we think the most significant contribution

grandparents can make in their grandchildren's lives is one that is spiritual in nature.

Paul wrote to his disciple Timothy, "I have been reminded of your sincere faith, which first lived in your grandmother Lois and in your mother Eunice and, I am persuaded, now lives in you also" (2 Tim 1:5). How did Timothy come to faith in Christ? It all began with his grandmother Lois. Who knows how many people have come to Christ through the prayers and gentle witness of a grandmother or grandfather.

The venerable apostle John wrote in his third epistle, "I have no greater joy than to hear that my children are walking in the truth" (3 Jn 4). He is speaking of his spiritual children, but the same could be said of our physical children. To a grandparent who is a believer, nothing is more thrilling than seeing a son, daughter or grandchild making wise choices and following Christ.

How can grandparents leave a spiritual legacy to their grandchildren? They can pray. There is nothing that will influence our grandchildren more than our prayers. There may be many times when you cannot be with your grandchildren physically or when your words alone may not influence them, but you can always reach them through prayer. Prayer is the secret weapon of every believer. Through prayer, you can minister to your grandchildren without their ever knowing it. Samuel declared to the people of Israel, "As for me, far be it from me that I should sin against the LORD by failing to pray for you" (1 Sam 12:23). Prayer is not dependent on physical proximity, a warm relationship with your children or children-in-law or your health. As long as we have life, regardless of our other circumstances, we can give our grandchildren the gift of our prayer support.

Grandparents may also have the privilege of sharing with their grandchildren what Christ means to them. A recent study showed that 80 percent of Christians make their decision for Christ before the age of eighteen. Of the remaining 20 percent, three-fourths say that their decision to follow Christ was greatly influenced by seeds sown before their eighteenth birthday. Grandparents can have a far-reaching ministry in their grandchildren's lives by sharing with them while they are young the difference Christ has made in their lives. If you love Christ, let your grandchildren see that you seek Christ's direction for the decisions you make. Show your grandchildren that God's Word is the authority you seek for all your decisions. Let your grandchildren hear you pray for your daily needs and for your family members, so that they see that you put your hope for security and strength in Christ. If you help your grandkids to know God personally, you are giving them a gift worth more than anything else. You are giving them a legacy that will endure for eternity.

Charlie Shedd writes:

Seminaries, graduate schools, Bible colleges, summer camps, weekend retreats—they've done their good. A lot of it maybe. Yet when it comes to theology in its purest form, can anything surpass this? A high school senior girl writes: "My grandmother makes me think that God is her best friend. I hope I can know him that way too."[6]

He goes on to tell about a thirteen-year-old boy named Timothy whose grandmother died. Cards of condolence were sent from many places to comfort the family, as were letters and telegrams. People dropped in by the dozen to offer words of comfort, and the phone rang constantly. But the thing which supported the family most were these unabashed words from Timothy:

Do you know what I like to think about now? It is how Grandma and I would sit and talk about heaven. She talked mostly about seeing Grandpa again. And her baby girl. Then we would discuss it. Would she still be a baby or grown now? And do you know what we decided? We decided heaven is how you want it.

Shedd adds, "Useless wondering? Maybe! Maybe not! Maybe it's one of the best reasons for being a grandpa or grandma."[7]

Jorie and I want our children to have these discussions with their grandparents. Some of them have had them already. And these are the discussions we look forward to having someday as grandparents. We wonder how many young people learn about God from their grandparents? We trust the number is very high. More than anything else, passing on a spiritual legacy requires grandparents who love the Lord.

Before his death, Joshua told the people of Israel of a decision he had made:

> Now fear the LORD and serve him with all faithfulness. Throw away the gods your forefathers worshiped beyond the River and in Egypt, and serve the LORD. But if serving the LORD seems undesirable to you, then choose for yourselves this day whom you will serve, whether the gods your forefathers served beyond the River, or the gods of the Amorites, in whose land you are living. But as for me and my household, we will serve the LORD (Josh 24:14-15).

If we want to pass God's commands on to our children or grandchildren, they must first be on our hearts. Before we can pass a spiritual legacy on to our children or grandchildren, we must first love the Lord with our whole heart. Is this true of you?

Questions for Reflection and Discussion

1. Read Psalm 128:5-6. Why is grandparenting considered a blessing of God?

2. Do you feel grandparents should offer to help with the grandchildren? Why or why not?

3. Of the five guidelines for grandparents to observe when helping with their grandchildren, which do you feel is the one most frequently violated?

4. Grandparents have the unique privilege of being nurturers to their grandchildren. Why is this such an important role?

5. How do you feel grandparents can best pass on a spiritual legacy?

6. What principle or insight in this chapter was most helpful to you?

9
Elderly
In-Laws

L*ate one Saturday at an Idaho race-*
track, a custodian, making his rounds to lock up, came upon an old man
sitting placidly in a wheelchair. He was wearing a brand-new sweatsuit,
blue bedroom slippers and a baseball cap inscribed with "Proud to Be
an American." A typewritten note identified him as "John King," a retired
farmer suffering from Alzheimer's disease.

In reality, the man was John Kingery, age eighty-two, a former auto
worker from Portland, Oregon. His daughter had apparently removed
him from a Portland nursing home and driven him three hundred miles
east, where she dumped him.

"Granny-dumping" is on the rise, say observers such as Robert Anzinger, past president of the American College of Emergency Physicians.

He estimates that between 100,000 and 200,000 elderly people are left on the doorsteps of hospitals every year. Whoever brought them there quickly sped away, leaving nurses and other staff to figure out identity, insurance coverage and a plan for the future.[1]

Although you may wonder how someone can do something so heartless to their own flesh and blood, such acts of desperation are on the rise, partly because people are growing older and living longer. By the end of this decade, the average life expectancy in the U.S. will be 80 years. In 1990, the oldest person on the U.S. Social Security rolls was a 136-year-old man named Charlie Smith. Those 85 and older make up the fastest-growing segment of the population in the U.S. During the past thirty years, while the overall U.S. population grew 39 percent, the ranks of those 85 and older jumped 232 percent. Since 1982, the number of people in the United States over age 65 has exceeded those under the age of 18. The over-55 population is multiplying three times faster than the population at large. The U.S. is moving from a youth-oriented culture to a nation of middle-aged and older adults. Housing for the elderly is expected to be a primary focus of the construction industry over the next two decades.[2]

As life expectancy has increased and the health of senior citizens has improved, programs for the elderly have become a growing concern. The American Society on Aging reports that by the year 2000, 65 percent of U.S. citizens will be over 65 years of age, and there will be six million people over 85! Adding together living parents, parents-in-law, stepparents and step-parents-in-law, the average American today has more parents than children.

The care of elderly parents or in-laws can become a source of tension in a marriage. We have witnessed many cases where a son-or daughter-in-law was resentful of having to care for his or her in-laws. Since people are living longer nowadays, it is wise for couples to discuss early in their marriage—or even before they get married—how they will deal with the care of elderly parents. Early discussion and agreement can help minimize in-law problems in this sensitive area of aging parents. How should families deal with the care of elderly parents and in-laws? We have three observations for children and one for elderly parents.

Principle Nine: Treat Elderly In-Laws with Dignity and Respect
The apostle Paul, in giving his young disciple Timothy advice on how to oversee the church in Ephesus, sets the standard that the elderly are to be treated with dignity. He instructs, "Do not rebuke an older man harshly, but exhort him as if he were your father. Treat younger men as brothers, older women as mothers" (1 Tim 5:1-2). In our culture, which has made gods of beauty and physical prowess, age becomes a liability. In contrast, God's Word insists that we show veneration for the elderly.

A member of our church shared with me that before he and his wife married they discussed the possibility of taking care of their parents in their old age. They agreed to either take them into their home or support them financially. They also determined that in the event that one of their parents lived with them, *they would make it work.* They decided they would demote their own needs to second place. They further agreed that no matter what happened, they would treat their parents with dignity.

If the time comes when there is a role reversal and children need to become parents to their parents and parents-in-law, it feels strange. It is difficult to find oneself in the role of parenting parents.

Trish was a single parent in her fifties. Her daughter, Wendy, was twenty-seven and lived with her. One evening Trish went on a date. She expected to return home right after the show, but she and her date decided to go out for a late dinner. When Trish opened the door at 1 a.m., the hall light came on. Standing before her was a very concerned daughter.

"Mother!" she exclaimed. "Where have you been? I was about to call the police!"

As Trish stood on the steps, she experienced a sudden flashback to herself in the same position years earlier. After she apologized to her daugher, the two had a good laugh about their temporary role reversals.[3]

In many cases, as parents age and lose physical and mental strength, role reversals between children and parents are permanent. As our parents and parents-in-law age, how we care for them will vary with our circumstances. As you consider what is best for your families and how to best honor your parents and parents-in-law, several steps may be helpful.

1. Assess the situation. Asking questions helps. What are their needs? What extended family support is available? What resources (finances, car, housing) are available? You also need to consider the needs of your immediate family. If you are struggling with toddlers or dual job schedules with little flexibility, options will be limited. If you are single or do not have children in the home, you may be more flexible.

In the vast majority of cases, parents and grown children prefer to live separately. Only one over-sixty-five person in ten is unable to be totally independent. Special problems present themselves when families must double up. The problems are not insurmountable, but they are a special challenge to carefully consider. Relationship difficulties are intensified by closeness.

When a mother or mother-in-law or father or father-in-law live with children, it's essential to work out space arrangements and areas of responsibility. If parents are physically able and you divide up responsibility for meal preparation, for example, each should have complete independence to spend the grocery money and prepare the food in his or her own way. Or if Grandmother lives in the home, she should have one room or space that she can furnish and arrange in her own way. It's all part of respecting each other's individuality. It's all part of fulfilling God's Word, which says, " 'Honor your father and mother'—which is the first commandment with a promise" (Eph 6:2).

There is no age limitation on this verse. Regardless of our age, we are all called to show respect to our parents. When different generations live under one roof, no person can demand that everything suit him or her. Everyone involved will need to muster as great an amount of flexibility as possible and to say "yes" as often as possible to reasonable requests. For example, if an older person's poor circulation requires more warmth, the thermostat can be set higher and the younger people can dress more lightly, or the older person can wear thermal underwear, or a safe way can be found to provide extra heat in the spot where the older person spends the most time.

2. Communicate clearly with your extended family as you make decisions about your aging parents. Working together to solve problems can be an opportunity for brothers and sisters to deepen their friendships if all are willing to be sensitive to each other in the process.

3. Treat elderly family members with honor. Scripture calls us to treat age with dignity. (See 1 Tim 5:2.) Doing so may at times require us to work hard at practicing patience; it may be inconvenient and time-consuming.

A sad story is told of an elderly man who lived with his son and daughter-in-law and their children. As he grew older, his hands began to shake with increasing frequency. At the dinner table, it was not uncommon for him to drop his fork, spill his drink or knock food onto the floor. His mealtime sloppiness irritated his son and daughter-in-law. They scolded him for his behavior and told him that they would make him eat out of a trough on the floor if he didn't stop slopping food on the table and floor. But even with their admonishing, he could not control his limbs. Finally, in anger, his son and daughter-in-law made good on their threat. They built a primitive trough and made their father eat his meals in a corner on the floor, without the aid of silverware.

After watching their grandfather's humiliation for several days, the grandchildren began a building project of their own. When their father found them working with hammers, boards and nails, he asked them what they were making. The kids replied proudly, "We're making a trough for you and Mom to eat out of when you get old!" The dad realized the terrible mistake he and his wife had made, and the grandfather was restored to his rightful place at the table that night.

Our children are watching the way we treat our parents and parents-in-law. The way they see us treat our parents may be the way they will treat us someday.

4. Be willing to make hard decisions about their care. Encourage your parents to make their own choices for their own care as long as possible. But the time may come when you need to step in. It is possible that you may have to make decisions even when they don't agree. This should be done only when it is obvious that the parents are unable to make their own decisions, and it should be done in a way to preserve the parents' dignity. They may think they can still drive a car when it is really no longer safe for them to do so. They may want to live alone, but that may not be wise. You may have to intervene for their safety and the safety of others.

5. Be willing to make personal sacrifices. We must be willing to sacrifice space in our home, financial resources and time to care for our parents. It may not be easy. But then again, we weren't easy to care for when we were young! Now it is our turn to honor them and care for them. Out of love for our spouse, we must be ready to help our in-laws, too. At this point in our lives, it is vitally important to have grafted our parents-in-law as true parents, and there should be no distinctions as to the love and concern we give to both sets of parents. Their situations, however, may need to be handled completely differently because of factors such as finances, other children, proximity and health.

One woman who had long struggled with her mother and her in-laws expressed concern when her husband was offered a great job in the town where her mom and in-laws lived. If they moved, she reasoned, her mother—who was old and all alone—would expect their attention. Her in-laws would also expect them to visit often. She was afraid to relocate to that town.

She was probably right about the pressures—but good can come out of hardship when we obey God. It might not always be convenient to have elderly parents, but love and respect demand that we make such sacrifices. It takes time, but it's also a privilege.

Elderly people can sense when we do not really care about them. A nurse who worked in geriatrics for twenty years understood the rejection so many senior citizens feel. She wrote this make-believe letter and sent it in to advice columnist Ann Landers.

Dear Caregiver,

I'm sorry you have to go through all this unpleasantness every day, and I regret that I am the cause of it. I hate not being able to do so many things for myself. It's awful to be totally dependent on someone else. I feel ashamed that I can't go to the bathroom on my own. It's frustrating to be fed by another person. I'm absolutely disgusted that I am unable to get a tissue up to my face so I can blow my nose. Being old and helpless is much worse than any illness or disability. It does things to one's feelings of personal worth. Worst of all is knowing how you hate being my caregiver. I see the resentment in your eyes and I hear it in your voice. I know that deep down you wish I would die and get it over with so you can get on with your life and not be bothered with me.

Well, I wish the same. Surprised? I have no choice, however, but to live out the years that have been allotted to me. I'm sorry that the job of caring for me has fallen on your shoulders. I wonder which of us carries the bigger burden.[4]

Would that none of us will ever feel that kind of resentment, but if you do, it's time to work on changing the circumstances that make you resentful. Some families think they can handle the closeness of living together or being caregivers for elderly parents—and find out they can't. They lovingly and willingly make personal sacrifices for their parents, but then they find it puts more wear and tear on their marriage or children or their own physical or emotional strength than they ever imagined. If this is true of you or someone you know, instead of buckling under the burden of stress and guilt, it's time to take three crucial steps: (1) backtrack and reassess; (2) honestly communicate; (3) look for alternate solutions. There are other sacrifices we can make on behalf of our parents to provide quality care for them other than being the caregivers ourselves. If we're resentful, it's very difficult to hide those feelings. We want to provide situations where we can show honor and respect to our aging parents.

A poem written by a woman who died in the geriatric ward of Ashludie Hospital near Dunde, England, was found among her possessions. It was addressed to the nurses who cared for her in her final days. Her words say a great deal about the worth and needs of the elderly. May it encourage you to spend more attention to your aging parents or parents-in-law.

What do you see, nurse, what do you see?
Are you thinking when you look at me—
A crabbed old woman, not very wise,
Uncertain of habit, with faraway eyes,

Who dribbles her food and makes no reply
When you say in a loud voice—
"I do wish you'd try."
Who seems not to notice the things that you do
And forever is losing a stocking or shoe,
Who resisting or not, lets you do as you will
With bathing and feeding, the long day to fill.
Is that what you're thinking, is that what you see?
Then open your eyes, nurse. You're not looking at me.
I'll tell you who I am as I sit here so still.
As I move at your bidding, eat at your will,
I'm a small child of ten with a father and mother,
Brothers and sisters who love one another;
A young girl of sixteen with wings on her feet,
Dreaming that soon a love she'll meet;
A bride at twenty, my heart gives a leap,
Remembering the vows that I promised to keep;
At twenty-five now I have young of my own
Who need me to build a secure, happy home.
A woman of thirty, my young now grow fast,
Bound together with ties that should last.
At forty, my young sons have grown up and gone,
But my man's beside me to see I don't mourn.
At fifty once more babies play round my knee—
Again we know children, my loved one and me.
Dark days are upon me, my husband is dead.
I look at the future, I shudder with dread.
For my young are all rearing young of their own,
And I think of the years and the love that I've known.
I'm an old woman now and nature is cruel.

'Tis her jest to make old age look like a fool.
The body it crumbles, grace and vigor depart.
There is a stone where I once had a heart.
But inside this old carcass a young girl still dwells,
And now again my bittered heart swells.
I remember the joys, I remember the pain
And I'm loving and living life over again.
I think of the years, all too few, gone too fast,
And accept the stark fact that nothing can last.
So open your eyes, nurse, open and see
Not a crabbed old woman,
Look closer—see me![5]

Let's be people who treat our parents and in-laws with dignity until their last day. Let's treat them the way we would want to be treated. Jesus has the final word to say on how we ought to treat our elderly parents or in-laws. "Do to others what you would have them do to you, for this sums up the Law and the Prophets" (Mt 7:12).

Prepare for No Regrets

When our parents and in-laws die, we want to look back with a sense of gratitude rather than regret. We want to be able to say without hesitation that we loved our in-laws to the best of our ability. The most difficult funerals I conduct are those where family members feel guilty for ways they mistreated the one who died. Most often this happens when the death came suddenly and there was no time to deal with unresolved business. If our parents and parents-in-law are still living, we can still make sure we straighten things out, ask for forgiveness if necessary, even start over.

Mr. Williams had a serious heart attack. In the hospital, he asked the nurse to call his only daughter and closest relative. So the nurse phoned the daughter. Hearing the news, the daughter burst into tears. She said, "But you don't understand. I haven't talked to my father in over a year. We had a terrible argument on my twenty-first birthday over my boyfriend. I ran out of the house and never went back. The last thing I said to my father was, 'I hate you.' "

But she said she would come to the hospital as soon as she could. The nurse went back to the room and thought about the tragedy of a father and daughter who were so lost to each other. Then, still waiting for the daughter to arrive, she noticed on the monitor that Mr. Williams had no pulse. She called a "code blue," and doctors rushed in to do everything possible to save his life—all to no avail. He was dead.

The nurse dreaded going out of that room and facing the daughter, who had arrived during all the commotion of the code blue. Outside the room, a doctor had already greeted the daughter and told her the dreaded news. The nurse noticed the deep hurt reflected on the girl's face and the tears in her eyes. Suddenly the girl whirled toward the nurse and pleaded, "I want to see my father." The nurse squeezed her hand, wishing she could dissuade her, but guided her to her dead father's side. In an effort not to intrude on the sad goodbye, the nurse backed against the bedside table, knocking a scrap of yellow paper off the table. She picked it up and read: "My dearest Janie, I forgive you. I pray you will also forgive me. I know that you love me. I love you too. Daddy." The nurse handed it to Janie. The daughter read it once; then read it again. Her tormented face grew radiant, and peace began to glisten in her eyes.[6]

Thank God that broken relationships, sometimes as fragile as snowflakes, can be put together again. But there is no time to spare. The apostle Paul admonishes us, "Get rid of all bitterness, rage and anger, brawling and slander, along with every form of malice. Be kind and compassionate to one another, forgiving each other, just as in Christ God forgave you" (Eph 4:31-32). Is there some family member you need to forgive or of whom you need to ask forgiveness? Are you bitter toward a mother-in-law or father-in-law? Are you withholding kindness toward a daughter-in-law or son-in-law? Have you been slandering a sister-in-law or brother-in-law? Don't delay. If you have someone with whom you need to reconcile, it's wise to mend that relationship while there is still time.

There are many small but significant things we can do to nurture relationships as parents and parents-in-law are aging. Some of our suggestions may be helpful to you as you consider what steps you can take right now.

1. Shop for your parents and in-laws. Shopping for grandchildren who are constantly growing, changing sizes and developing new interests can be a daunting task. Although our parents used to do all the gift shopping for the grandchildren themselves, in the last few years both of our mothers have preferred sending us a check and asking us to do the shopping. Other seniors find it helpful, as they grow older, when children or grandchildren can do their grocery shopping or pick up necessities like stamps and light bulbs for them.

2. Ask about the past. Jorie's dad is eighty-five years old. Often he can remember a detail about his growing-up years better than what he had for lunch that day. He loves talking about his first car, the price of candy when he grew up and what it was like during the Great Depression. Asking him about the past provides a great opportunity for us to learn about an earlier generation and enables him to recall significant childhood or adulthood memories.

We also find that asking about the past is good for our children. One of our boys was writing a report for school about what life was like in the 1920s and 1930s. He called my dad and Jorie's mother and interviewed them with a set of questions provided for him by his teacher. Our parents did some research, and each wrote him long letters giving him a lot of information about what life was like when they grew up. Our parents enjoyed helping him, and our boy was able to turn in a good report. And these reports are safely stored away for the future in that grandson's "treasure box." Other families make audio or video tapes of their parents' memory-telling or take trips together to learn of their roots and trace their family trees. The main connection with our family history is our parents, and they can provide a wealth of information and fun for us and our children.

3. Downshift to a slower pace. We live on a high-octane schedule of soccer and basketball games, tennis tournaments, swim meets, piano lessons, drama rehearsals, school activities, youth group functions, birthday parties, church programs, speaking engagements and writing deadlines. When our parents visit and see the whirl of activity at our house, they roll their eyes in wonderment at how we handle it all. We can hardly expect them to adopt our breakneck schedule. So we downshift to a little slower pace when we are together—and love it.

This step may require some advance planning. But even for a child who agrees to give up a certain activity in order to devote part of an afternoon to being Grandma's companion, the tradeoff may prove a valuable one.

4. Provide physical help. Many parents and parents-in-law prefer to stay in their own homes as long as they are able, but many need increasing assistance with tasks that become more difficult for them. Providing help like offering to mow the lawn, rake leaves or clean gutters may be welcomed, as may putting up and taking down a Christmas tree or cleaning carpets. Each family's needs and capabilities are different, but thoughtful children and grandchildren will look for ways to help.

5. Travel together. Some of our best times with our in-laws have come when we have taken trips together. Vacations when we are all removed from pressing schedules and personal responsibilites enable in-laws to spend enjoyable times together and engage in relaxed communication. What great memories we are building during these times!

6. *Stay in touch.* Even if you do not live near your in-laws and cannot visit often, you can stay in touch through regular letters or phone calls. There is almost no excuse for not keeping in steady phone contact these days. The calls need not be long—just enough to stay in communication. A short call can be the highlight of an elderly parent's day. We have lived on the west coast for twenty years, while Jorie's family has remained in the Midwest. Yet never a week has passed when Jorie has not talked with her parents on the phone, and each year we and our kids have flown back to the Midwest for a visit. Staying in touch can be expensive, but the relationship is definitely worth it.

A less expensive and thoroughly up-to-date way to stay in touch nowadays is through e-mail. One friend shared with us that this is the method she and her husband use to stay in touch with her grandfather, who loves computers. It's much cheaper than a phone call and allows him to hear from them very regularly. They have group lists on the e-mail so that letters are circulated to Grandpa and the aunts and cousins; e-mail, in fact, has helped them reconnect with relatives they had been out of touch with for years.

Seek Mentoring from Parents-in-Law

One of the reasons God has put us together in families is so that parents can teach their children and prepare them for the best possible life. Likewise, parents-in-law provide adult children a fine opportunity for being mentored. Scripture is replete with examples of people who were older and wiser in the faith discipling those who were younger in their relationship with Christ. Paul discipled Timothy. Barnabas encouraged

Paul. Hilkiah, the high priest, instructed young Josiah, who became king of Judah when he was only eight years old.

The apostle Paul tells older women to teach younger women:

Likewise, teach the older women to be reverent in the way they live, not to be slanderers or addicted to much wine, but to teach what is good. Then they can train the younger women to love their husbands and children, to be self-controlled and pure, to be busy at home, to be kind, and to be subject to their husbands, so that no one will malign the word of God. (Tit 2:3-5)

A mentor is someone further down the road from us who is going where we want to go and who is willing to show us how to get there. The usual distinction between discipling and mentoring is this: discipling is more formal. Mentoring is informal. Mentoring happens over a cup of coffee or while we're preparing a meal, changing a bed or fixing a car. It is one of God's finest methods for teaching his people. Men and women need mentors.

I have had a half-dozen or more mentors in my lifetime. These were people who were further along in their marriage, faith or ministry than I was. The process has been the same in every case. I came to them and asked questions such as "How do you do this? What do you do in this situation? Why do you do it that way?" Every time, I found they were more than happy to help me. In fact, I think they appreciated being asked. In almost every case, we came to consider each other the best of friends. Not because we were peers, but because I asked all kinds of questions. People like it when someone admires them enough to ask questions of them. So do mothers- and fathers-in-law.

Mentoring will work best if daughters- or sons-in-law take the initiative. We've discussed how wise mothers- and fathers-in-law refrain from giving unsolicited advice. However, if they are asked their opinion, they are usually more than happy to share. And mentoring is not exclusive to Christians. A nonbeliever may still have lots of experience to share that can be of value to us.

It may begin with something as simple as a request for help in putting on a dinner party or decorating your home. If your mate and his or her siblings are well-adjusted and God-fearing, you may want to ask your mother-in-law how she managed to raise such fine children, all of whom have a heart for the Lord.

This question was asked of a mother whose boys were godly but whose husband was an atheist. The incredulous questioner wondered how such a thing could happen. The mother answered, "I can't say anything at home. I've never been able to. So I pray. Oh, do I pray! For an hour on my knees, every morning."[7]

If you are a son-in-law or daughter-in-law, when was the last time you asked your mother- or father-in-law for advice? Not being too proud to ask questions can open the door to a stronger relationship. You will probably benefit from the information you receive, and more than likely it will improve your relationship with your in-laws.

Parents, if your son- or daughter-in-law or your married child asks you a question, it will probably be wise to resist the temptation to unload everything you know in response to one question! And certainly don't turn a question into an invitation to reprimand or criticize. If you do, it will be a long time before you hear another question. It may be wise to resist the temptation to give children and children-in-law advice on how you would run things, spend money, raise kids and so on, unless they have specifically asked for it. If you have given advice and your children or children-in-law don't do what they know you expect them to do, they may feel guilty and it may hurt your relationship.

An important phrase to use with your children might be, "Listen to what I say, and then do as you please." This assurance gives you free-dom to offer your children and children-in-law advice based on your experience, yet it assures them they are free make their own decisions without getting further unsolicited advice or an "I-told-you-so" attitude from you. When in doubt as to whether you should give advice, it's probably safer to remain silent. Whenever you are asked your opinion, tell them you are happy to give it, but make sure you communicate once again that you support your children and trust them to make their own decisions.

One woman writes of her mother-in-law's great caution in this delicate area of giving advice:

Mom has never interfered in our lives. She has never suggested how we should live. She has worried about us, but she supports us even when I am sure she thinks we are totally nuts.

Another woman told me that she was drawn to come to her mother-in-law for counsel because of her mother-in-law's respectful attitude toward her. She writes:

I cannot express how invaluable it has been for me to be able to ask my mother-in-law to pray about something in my life. She absolutely never pries, never gives personal opinions without being asked and never is judgmental or downgrading, despite all the times that I certainly deserved a good reprimand. Both she and my father-in-law have only said positive things about our parenting skills, our children, and our family life, and that positive reinforcement has been water to my dry roots on many occasions.

Mentoring can be mutually fulfilling to the parents and parents-in-law who give it and the children and children-in-law who receive it, if children take the initiative to ask and parents answer sensitively without concern about whether or not their advice is implemented. When the mentoring is done out of mutual love, children can benefit immensely from the experience and expertise of their parents and parents-in-law.

And now a word to parents and parents-in-law.

Here is an important piece of advice as you look ahead to the changes retirement and aging will bring: *Take responsibility for making your senior years happy and productive.*

Once in a while we meet grandparents who embrace the attitude that their children owe them happiness. Sometimes we hear comments like: "My children don't visit me much anymore," or "My kids are so busy, they don't have time for me anymore." Psychologists call this kind of behavior "passive manipulation." Those of us who have married children need to remember that heaping guilt on them for neglecting our own well-being and happiness will not draw them in love to us. It may actually do the opposite and drive them away. Many seniors live with incredible hardship, including the financial restraints of fixed pensions, debilitating illnesses and the death of their mates and lifetime friends. Some people feel cheated and are tempted to blame God or others for the misfortune of their circumstances.

There's no hint in the Bible that happiness can ever come from blaming other people for our circumstances or for manipulating others into meeting our demands and conforming to our wishes. Happiness is not something someone else can give to us. No one else can make us happy. We have to figure out how to make ourselves happy in our circumstances.

Scripture teaches that happiness is a byproduct of knowing Christ. Paul says, "Rejoice in the Lord always. I will say it again: Rejoice!" (Phil 4:4). Referring to God, Solomon asks, "For without him, who can eat or find enjoyment?" (Eccl 2:25). True joy comes from knowing the God who made us and obeying his commands. Our part is to pursue worthwhile goals and to fill our minds with the right thoughts. In addition, we need to ask God to help us shape our feelings and attitudes into what they ought to be. And along the way, as we work on these things, we will discover, amazingly, that we're happy! We must find our own happiness through our relationships with Christ, our mate and our friends. We dare not sit around expecting our children and grandchildren to fulfill our needs.

As we seek happiness independent of our children and grandchildren, we may find our relationships with our children and grandchildren are more rewarding. A delightful senior-citizen friend of ours with three children and six grandchildren told us of a trip she and her husband took to Knott's Berry Farm. Guess what she told us when she returned home? Her favorite ride was called the Big Foot Raft Ride. It is a huge tire with six seats. The raft is propelled down a narrow canal by a rapidly flowing current. As it careens down the channel, water splashes over the passengers. The big thrill of the ride is when it goes under an enormous waterfall. Since the tire is constantly spinning, no one can quite predict which of the riders will get most drenched.

What interested us most was not that she went on the ride, but that she rode it three times in a row! She got completely drenched and loved it! And can you imagine how much fun her grandsons had, watching their grandma get soaked? That's living life to the fullest. Does reaching her stage in life mean she can never do anything daring or childlike? No way!

It's possible that our senior years can be the most fun and meaningful of all. We may have more time to nurture the relationships we have with our sons and sons-in-law, daughters and daughters-in-law and grandchildren than we've had at any other point in our lives. Jorie's and my parents have each had wonderful times taking trips and enjoying all kinds of wonderful activities with our children.

As we take responsibility for our own happiness, we may also find that our senior years become the most productive years of our lives. Many so-called "senior citizens" today are rejecting the retirement mentality. They are extending their careers or launching new ones; they are getting involved in exciting new ministries.

Several years ago I received a telephone call from Bartlett Hess, pastor of the 5,000-member Ward Presbyterian Church in Livonia, Michigan. He was eighty-one at the time. He told me it was time for him to step down and turn the church over to new leadership. He was looking for his replacement.

"Are you going to retire?" I asked.

"Oh no," he replied. "I'm going to start a new church." At eighty-one!

In *The Power of Optimism*, Alan Loy McGinnis tells how Harry Lipsig, at age eighty-eight, decided to leave the New York law firm he had spent most of sixty years building up (and where he was earning $5 million a year) to open a new firm. There had been some differences with his younger partners, who questioned his ability to handle lengthy court trials. (One judge recalled Mr. Lipsig saying that he wasn't dying fast enough for his partners.) So in 1988, Mr. Lipsig decided to personally try his first case in some time. Here is the *Wall Street Journal*'s analysis:

The plaintiff was suing the city of New York because a drunken police officer had struck and killed her 71-year-old husband with his patrol car. She was . . . arguing that the city had deprived her of her husband's future earning potential. The city argued that at age 71, he had little earning potential. What better evidence for the plaintiff than the presence in court of a vigorous 88-year-old attorney? The city settled the case for $1.25 million.

When asked about retirement, Harry responded, "Retire? Never. A few doctors have recommended it along the way," he noted with a smile, "but they're all dead now."[8]

A study of Harvard University graduates at age 75 yielded a surprising result. Among 100 men who had retired at 65, seven out of eight were dead by age 75. In a second group of 100 who had worked beyond 65, only one in eight had died by age 75. The researchers concluded that retiring too early in life significantly reduces one's longevity.[9]

Seniors who lead happy and productive lives are like a man named Caleb whom we read about in Joshua 14. The people of Israel had just settled in the Promised Land and were still in the process of conquering the land. At eighty-five, Caleb came to Joshua and asked for the hill country around Hebron, which God had promised him over forty years earlier, when he returned from spying out the land and reported that the Israelites could conquer if they trusted in God. He says:

Now then, just as the LORD promised, he has kept me alive for forty-five years since the time he said this to Moses, while Israel moved about in the desert. So here I am today, eighty-five years old! I am still as strong today as the day Moses sent me out; I'm just as vigorous to go out to battle now as I was then. Now give me this hill country that the LORD promised me that day. You yourself heard then that the Anakites were there and their cities were large and fortified, but, the LORD helping me, I will drive them out just as he said (Josh 14:10-12).

In chapter 15 we read that Caleb drove out all of the Anakites. What an account! Here's a man who is eighty-five years old. Has he been warehoused in retirement? No way! He's as gutsy and determined and robust as he was at forty. He's not thinking about dying. He's focused on living! We all need to focus on living.

Some members of a retirement home said to a pastor, "We love it when you come." "Why?" he asked. "Well," they replied, "when others come, they tell us how to get ready to die. When you come, you tell us how to get ready to live."

If you are in your senior years or nearing retirement, consider your retirement carefully. It may be beneficial, if health and work policy allow, to work beyond age sixty-five. Or get involved in ministry and in the lives of your grandchildren—get so busy that it doesn't feel like you are retired at all. You'll enjoy life more if you're involved in meaningful work and ministry; you'll probably experience a better relationship with your children, children-in-law and grandchildren; odds are, you'll live longer.

* * *

A Final Word

Although we believe that following the principles we have set forth in this book will greatly improve your relationship with your in-laws, it would be simplistic to suggest that these insights will bring an instant cure to every struggling in-law relationship. It may not be possible to establish strong bonds where alcoholism, drug abuse, sexual abuse or other damaging patterns are factors in the relationship. In such cases, we can only pray for God to rescue the in-law from bondage before we can begin to build the relationship. There may be other in-law relationships where deep-seated psychological and emotional needs need to be met before there can be much hope of building a meaningful relationship with the in-law. In such cases, sadly, we have had to counsel individuals to keep their contacts to a minimum and simply be as civil as possible toward their in-laws.

One woman whom we counseled regarding her relationship with her in-laws wrote to us:

My situation with my in-laws has not improved much, probably because I do not desire to spend time with them. It just seems to work better that way. There is still a lot of resentment on my part and on my mother-in-law's part, judging from the struggles we experience when we are together.

This woman has come to the disappointing conclusion that her relationship with her in-laws will probably never be very good. In some cases, resigning ourselves to expect limited results in our relationship with in-laws helps us cope better than having our relational attempts meet with constant rejection.

Yes, it's all too clear that in-law relationships are some of the most difficult of all relationships to cultivate.

God has given us in-laws, however, to broaden our perspective, to provide us with rich friendships that will help us in the lifelong process of becoming more like him. It's worth the effort! We must put into practice the principles of love, healthy self-esteem, leaving parents, cleaving to our spouses, trusting in God's sovereignty, communicating the truth in love, managing and channeling our anger, using grandparenting as an opportunity to nurture grandchildren, and treating elderly in-laws with respect. If we do this, we have a far better chance of fostering rewarding relationships with our in-laws.

We have grown in the process of writing this book, and we hope it has been of help to you, as well.

Questions for Reflection and Discussion

1. Robert Anzinger estimates that between 100,000 and 200,000 elderly people are left on the doorsteps of hospitals every year. Why do you suppose "granny-dumping" is on the rise?

2. Do you think it is important that couples, before marrying, discuss their convictions about taking care of their parents in their old age? Why or why not?

3. Do you think it is a good idea for children to take elderly parents into their home to live with them? When do you feel it is appropriate, and what might be a case when it would be inappropriate?

4. If someone approached you for advice on how to mend his or her relationship with an estranged parent, what would you counsel? What guidance do you find in Ephesians 4:31-32, Philippians 2:1-5 and Philippians 4:2-3?

5. Read Ecclesiastes 12:1-13. What advice for seniors do you find in these verses?

6. What principle or insight in this chapter was most helpful to you?

Notes

Chapter 1: How Problems Begin
[1]Ann Landers, *Oregonian,* February 23, 1995.
[2]Jean Parvin, "Do Your In-Laws Drive You Crazy?" *Reader's Digest,* May 1995, p. 166.
[3]Ibid., pp. 165-66.
[4]Mark R. Littleton, in "Laughter, the Best Medicine," *Reader's Digest,* April 1982, p. 79.

Chapter 2: Love: The Key That Unlocks the Door
[1]Natasha Josefowitz, "The People My Children Married," in *Natasha's Words for Lovers* (New York: Warner Books, 1986), p. 62.
[2]Dee Brestin, *The Friendships of Women* (Wheaton, Ill.: Victor Books, 1988), pp. 151-52.
[3]Claudia Arp, "Being the Best Mother-in-Law You Can Be," *Today's Christian Woman,* May/June 1994, pp. 51-54.
[4]Marie Greiser, in "Life in These United States," *Reader's Digest,* February 1978, p. 76.
[5]Author unknown.

Chapter 3: Healthy Self-Esteem: A Necessity for Love
[1]Cited by Larry G. Day in *By Design and in God's Image* (Portland, Ore.: Mt. Tabor Press, 1992), p. 22.
[2]Josh McDowell, *Building Your Self-Image* (Wheaton, Ill.: Tyndale House, 1984), p. 28.
[3]Many of these and others cited in ibid., pp. 53-55.
[4]Ibid., p. 116.
[5]*Leadership,* Summer 1990, p. 69.
[6]Paul Lewis, "How Shall We Teach Honesty?" *Dads Only* 3, no. 1 (January 1980): 1.
[7]Ted Miller, *Being a Caring Father* (San Francisco: Harper & Row, 1983), p. 87.

Chapter 4: Leaving & Cleaving
[1]Parvin, "Do Your In-Laws Drive You Crazy?" p. 170.
[2]Abigail Van Buren, "Dear Abby," *Oregonian,* March 7, 1995, p. C-3.
[3]*The Social Organization of Sexuality,* cited by Philip Elmer-Dewitt, "Now for the Truth About Americans and SEX," *Time,* October 17, 1994, pp. 62-70.

[4]Meredith, *Becoming One,* pp. 217-18.

Chapter 5: Beating the Urge to Control
[1]T. Berry Brazelton, "Who's Right?" *Family Circle,* June 28, 1994, p. 72.

Chapter 6: Communication
[1]Parvin, "Do Your In-Laws Drive You Crazy?" p. 170.
[2]Abigail Van Buren, "Dear Abby," *Oregonian,* March 8, 1995, p. E-2.

Chapter 7: Pulling the Plug on Anger
[1]Charles R. Swindoll, *Anger* (Portland, Ore.: Multnomah Press, 1981), p. 3.
[2]Gary Smalley and John Trent, *Home Remedies* (Portland, Ore.: Multnomah Press, 1991), p. 104.
[3]Tim LaHaye, *Spirit-Controlled Temperament* (Wheaton, Ill.: Tyndale House, 1966), p. 77.
[4]Larry Crabb, *The Marriage Builder* (Grand Rapids, Mich.: Zondervan, 1992), p. 71.
[5]Smalley and Trent, *Home Remedies,* p. 108.

Chapter 8: Grandparenting
[1]T. Berry Brazelton, "Grandparents' Do's and Don'ts," *Family Circle,* June 28, 1994, p. 74.
[2]Ibid., p. 75.
[3]Charlie Shedd, *Then God Created Grandparents* (Garden City, N.Y.: Doubleday, 1976), p. 93.
[4]Anon.
[5]Anon.
[6]Shedd, *Then God Created Grandparents,* p. 138.
[7]Ibid., p. 140.

Chapter 9: Elderly In-Laws
[1]Barbara Crosley, "Enjoy Your Elderly Parents," *Focus on the Family,* December 1992, p. 12.
[2]Win Arn, "Riding the Wave of Silver and Gray," *Leadership,* Fall 1990, p. 112.
[3]Susan Yates, "When In-Laws Are in Town," *Focus on the Family,* April 1995, p. 7.
[4]Ann Landers, *Oregonian,* February 28, 1988, p. C-2.
[5]Rolf Zettersten, "Close Encounters of the Best Kind," *Focus on the Family,* February 1991, p. 14.
[6]Sue Monk Kidd, "Don't Let It End This Way," *Guideposts,* 1979. Excerpted with permission from *Guideposts* Magazine. © 1979 by Guideposts, Carmel, NY 10512.
[7]Brestin, *The Friendships of Women,* p. 153.
[8]*Wall Street Journal,* June 12, 1989, cited by Alan Loy McGinnis in *The Power of Optimism* (San Francisco: Harper & Row, 1990), pp. 107-8.
[9]Larry Burkett, "Money Sense" *Moody,* April 1991, p. 34.